Learning Bootstrap

Unearth the potential of Bootstrap to create responsive
web pages using modern techniques

Aravind Shenoy

Ulrich Sossou

PACKT PUBLISHING

open source
community experience distilled

BIRMINGHAM - MUMBAI

Learning Bootstrap

First published: December 2014

Production reference: 1171214

Published by Packt Publishing Ltd.
Livery Place
35 Livery Street
Birmingham B3 2PB, UK.

ISBN 978-1-78216-184-4

www.packtpub.com

Credits

Authors
Aravind Shenoy
Ulrich Sossou

Reviewers
Ravi Kumar Gupta
Harsh Raval
Fred Sarmento

Acquisition Editor
Sam Wood

Content Development Editor
Amey Varangaonkar

Technical Editors
Tanvi Bhatt
Siddhi Rane

Copy Editors
Merilyn Pereira
Stuti Srivastava

Project Coordinator
Leena Purkait

Proofreaders
Bridget Braund
Maria Gould
Amy Johnson

Indexer
Priya Sane

Production Coordinator
Shantanu N. Zagade

Cover Work
Shantanu N. Zagade

About the Authors

Aravind Shenoy is an in-house author at Packt Publishing. An engineering graduate from the Manipal Institute of Technology, his core interests lie in technical writing, web designing, and software testing. He was born, and is based, in Mumbai, India. A music buff, he loves listening to Oasis, R.E.M, The Doors, Dire Straits, and U2. Rock n' Roll and Rap rule his playlists. He is also the author of several other books such as *Thinking in HTML* and *Hadoop Explained,* both by Packt Publishing. You can find out more about him on the Amazon Author Central page at http://www.amazon.com/Aravind-Shenoy/e/B00ITSR2WE.

He can be contacted at aravind.shenoy@hotmail.com.

I would like to thank my uncle, Dr. Ramanath N. Kamath, for motivating me on this journey of writing the Bootstrap book. Also, a big thanks and deep gratitude to Edward Gordon and Julian Ursell from Packt Publishing, who helped me gain focus and precision in my writing abilities.

Ulrich Sossou is an experienced software engineer and entrepreneur with a passion for solving problems. He enjoys helping individuals and businesses frame difficult issues in ways that foster the emergence of the best outcomes for them and/or their businesses.

His first experience with technology came at age 8 in his uncle's computer repair shop, where he played with early versions of personal computers, such as the Macintosh Classic. Since then, he has gained valuable experience in software engineering, architecture, and design as well as marketing and sales, and he has developed the overall skill set required to run a software business.

When he's not working on open source projects or coaching less experienced software engineers or entrepreneurs, he's the CTO of Retreat Guru (`http://retreatguru.com/`), a Canadian company operating in the wellness tourism industry; the cofounder of Flyerco (`https://www.flyerco.com/`), an American company helping realtors market their properties with flyers; and the cofounder of TekXL (`http://www.tekxl.com/`), a west-African start-up incubator.

About the Reviewers

Ravi Kumar Gupta is an open source software evangelist and Liferay expert. He pursued the MS degree in Software System from BITS Pilani and BTech from LNMIIT, Jaipur. His technological forte is portal management and development using Liferay.

He is currently working as a senior consultant with CIGNEX Datamatics. He was a core member of the Open Source Group at TCS, where he started working on Liferay and other UI technologies. During his career, he has been involved in building enterprise solutions using latest technologies with rich user interfaces and open source tools.

He loves to spend time writing, learning, and discussing new technologies. He is an active member of the Liferay forum. He also writes technical articles for his blog at TechD of Computer World (http://techdc.blogspot.in). He has been a Liferay trainer at TCS and CIGNEX, where he has trained on Liferay 5.x and 6.x versions.

He can be reached on Skype at kravigupta and on Twitter at @kravigupta. Connect with him on LinkedIn at http://in.linkedin.com/in/kravigupta.

I would like to thank my lovely wife and my family for their support. All that I am is because of them. Their support helped me through good and bad times. I would also like to thank my friends and colleagues for their support.

Harsh Raval is a passionate self-taught software developer with many years of experience. He is a part-time blogger and blogs about various technologies and his experiences. He holds a Bachelor's degree in Computer Science.

He started his carrier as a backend engineer, working on various backend frameworks, mostly in Java. Now he also has experience and expertise in frontend technologies. He started coding frontend development as a hobby and ended up designing and implementing beautiful backend and frontend systems using the various JavaScript frameworks out there.

> As this is the first book that I am a part of, I dedicate this to my family.

Fred Sarmento is a frontend developer and UI designer based in Lisbon, Portugal. He has more than 5 years of experience in this field, and has been working with some great New York and San Francisco start-ups. In 2014, he founded Cropfection (www.cropfection.com), a company that provides frontend consultancy and development.

www.PacktPub.com

Support files, eBooks, discount offers, and more

For support files and downloads related to your book, please visit www.PacktPub.com.

Did you know that Packt offers eBook versions of every book published, with PDF and ePub files available? You can upgrade to the eBook version at www.PacktPub.com and as a print book customer, you are entitled to a discount on the eBook copy. Get in touch with us at service@packtpub.com for more details.

At www.PacktPub.com, you can also read a collection of free technical articles, sign up for a range of free newsletters and receive exclusive discounts and offers on Packt books and eBooks.

https://www2.packtpub.com/books/subscription/packtlib

Do you need instant solutions to your IT questions? PacktLib is Packt's online digital book library. Here, you can search, access, and read Packt's entire library of books.

Why subscribe?
- Fully searchable across every book published by Packt
- Copy and paste, print, and bookmark content
- On demand and accessible via a web browser

Free access for Packt account holders

If you have an account with Packt at www.PacktPub.com, you can use this to access PacktLib today and view nine entirely free books. Simply use your login credentials for immediate access.

Table of Contents

Preface

Bootstrap is a powerful framework to empower and enhance frontend web designing. Version 3 comes with a plethora of features including a mobile-first responsive grid, LESS variables, tailor-made components, and plugins that help users design dynamic user interfaces. With the advent of mobile web development, owing to the fact that mobiles and tablets are increasingly becoming the de facto standard for using the Internet, it is essential that websites are developed from a mobile-first perspective and then adapted to larger screens for desktops and notebooks. Bootstrap is batteries-loaded meaning that it packs it all with expertly crafted solutions and attributes that help developers to accomplish difficult tasks with ease and greater speed. Apart from its built-in features, it gets vibrant support from the community mainly in terms of additional resources and third-party utilities that take out a great deal of guesswork when it comes to difficult layout styles resulting in enterprise-grade and aesthetic web applications. *Learning Bootstrap* is a comprehensive source to help you get to grips with the technical know-how enabling you to know the ins and outs of Bootstrap in an easy-to-follow format.

What this book covers

Chapter 1, Getting Started with Bootstrap, is a short introduction to the technology. This chapter explains the need for Bootstrap in addition to explaining the paradigm related to the mobile-first approach adopted by Bootstrap to streamline web designing.

Chapter 2, Installing and Customizing Bootstrap, discusses the inclusion of Bootstrap with relevant information, overriding with customized styles, the deep customization of Bootstrap, and compiling LESS files in a practical manner.

Chapter 3, Using the Bootstrap Grid, starts with usage of the Bootstrap Grid classes wherein you learn about adding rows and columns and offsets, nesting of columns, and using the different variables and mixins and summing it up with a real-time example of creating a custom blog layout.

Chapter 4, Using the Base CSS, builds up from explaining the typography and subsequently moves on to explain the various facets of CSS including tables, forms, buttons, and the various responsive utilities in a step-by-step approach also including the helper classes used extensively in Bootstrap.

Chapter 5, Adding Bootstrap Components, incorporates the learning of the popular components such as the Glyphicons and Breadcrumbs in addition to the different navigation components such as nav tabs, nav pills, and dropdowns, which help you to build interactive webpages.

Chapter 6, Doing More with Components, contains an extensive in-depth understanding of the remaining components such as wells, labels, progress bars, badges, panels, alerts, and pagination, which form a crux of modern websites enabling you to build aesthetic websites.

Chapter 7, Enhancing User Experience with JavaScript, deals with official and optional plugins to create modals, carousels, tooltips, and accordion, which empowers you to develop dynamic webpages in a jiffy thereby eliminating the need to write exhaustive and humongous code for those attributes.

Chapter 8, Bootstrap Technical Hub – A One-stop Shop for Powerful Bootstrap Utilities, helps you to leverage the benefits of third-party toolkits and themes tailored to streamline your web designing experience with Bootstrap. This section is a one-stop solution to a plethora of relevant resources such as templates, custom layouts, and code snippets that enable to build robust user interfaces in quick time and with minimum effort. It also includes an overview of the future of Bootstrap, the next steps, and the myriad compatibility with WordPress, Joomla, and the likes of it which make an imperative framework for futuristic web design.

Bonus Chapter, Building an E-Commerce Website with Bootstrap, describes the procedure to build a modern e-commerce website in a step-by-step format, which will help you to understand the web designing aspects in a real-world scenario. This bonus chapter is a sample example for readers who want to leverage the knowledge gained to build enterprise-level websites with relative ease in a systematic and efficient manner. This chapter can be found online at `https://www.packtpub.com/sites/default/files/downloads/Building%20an%20e-commerce%20Website%20with%20Bootstrap.pdf`.

What you need for this book

Apart from the basic fundamentals of HTML, CSS, and JavaScript, you would need an editor such as Notepad or Notepad++ to work with the examples in this book. Though we have written most of the code in Notepad, you may prefer to use Notepad++ as it is open source, advanced, and is loaded with features such as syntax highlighting and syntax folding, which help you code in a well organized way.

Who this book is for

Learning Bootstrap is for budding as well as proficient web designers and developers who want to build professional-looking, dynamic websites. Basic knowledge of HTML, HTML5, and CSS in addition to a little bit of JavaScript (very basic) is required for aspiring users looking to implement Bootstrap in their development process. Prior knowledge of Bootstrap is not needed as the learning guide equips you with all the know-how required to incorporate Bootstrap into your pet projects.

Conventions

In this book, you will find a number of text styles that distinguish between different kinds of information. Here are some examples of these styles and an explanation of their meaning.

Code words in text, database table names, folder names, filenames, file extensions, pathnames, dummy URLs, user input, and Twitter handles are shown as follows: "You will find that we have used the minified versions, that is, `bootstrap.min.js` and `bootstrap.min.css`, to lower the file size resulting in faster loading of the website."

A block of code is set as follows:

```
#packt   {
  padding: 19px 30px;
    -webkit-border-radius: 35px;
    -moz-border-radius: 35px;
  border-radius: 35px;
  color: red
}
```

When we wish to draw your attention to a particular part of a code block, the relevant lines or items are set in bold:

```
#packt    {
  padding: 19px 30px;
    -webkit-border-radius: 35px;
    -moz-border-radius: 35px;
  border-radius: 35px;
  color: red
}
```

Any command-line input or output is written as follows:

```
lessc --yui-compress bootstrap.less > bootstrap.min.css
```

New terms and **important words** are shown in bold. Words that you see on the screen, for example, in menus or dialog boxes, appear in the text like this: "Click on the **Download Bootstrap** button and the file will be downloaded in the ZIP format."

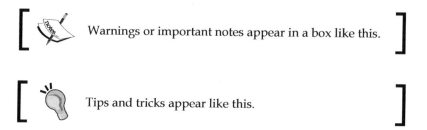

> Warnings or important notes appear in a box like this.

> Tips and tricks appear like this.

Reader feedback

Feedback from our readers is always welcome. Let us know what you think about this book—what you liked or disliked. Reader feedback is important for us as it helps us develop titles that you will really get the most out of.

To send us general feedback, simply e-mail feedback@packtpub.com, and mention the book's title in the subject of your message.

If there is a topic that you have expertise in and you are interested in either writing or contributing to a book, see our author guide at www.packtpub.com/authors.

Customer support

Now that you are the proud owner of a Packt book, we have a number of things to help you to get the most from your purchase.

Downloading the example code

You can download the example code files from your account at `http://www.packtpub.com` for all the Packt Publishing books you have purchased. If you purchased this book elsewhere, you can visit `http://www.packtpub.com/support` and register to have the files e-mailed directly to you.

Errata

Although we have taken every care to ensure the accuracy of our content, mistakes do happen. If you find a mistake in one of our books—maybe a mistake in the text or the code—we would be grateful if you could report this to us. By doing so, you can save other readers from frustration and help us improve subsequent versions of this book. If you find any errata, please report them by visiting `http://www.packtpub.com/submit-errata`, selecting your book, clicking on the **Errata Submission Form** link, and entering the details of your errata. Once your errata are verified, your submission will be accepted and the errata will be uploaded to our website or added to any list of existing errata under the Errata section of that title.

To view the previously submitted errata, go to `https://www.packtpub.com/books/content/support` and enter the name of the book in the search field. The required information will appear under the **Errata** section.

Piracy

Piracy of copyrighted material on the Internet is an ongoing problem across all media. At Packt, we take the protection of our copyright and licenses very seriously. If you come across any illegal copies of our works in any form on the Internet, please provide us with the location address or website name immediately so that we can pursue a remedy.

Please contact us at `copyright@packtpub.com` with a link to the suspected pirated material.

We appreciate your help in protecting our authors and our ability to bring you valuable content.

Questions

If you have a problem with any aspect of this book, you can contact us at `questions@packtpub.com`, and we will do our best to address the problem.

1
Getting Started with Bootstrap

The styling and presentation of your website is imperative, as it plays an important role in creating a sublime user experience. Therefore, you need to acquire design skills, which help you to create attractive websites. Add deadlines to the project where time is imperative and you realize you have quite a task at hand. Several toolkits and frameworks have come to the fore to ease and streamline the task of web designing but none comes close to the open source framework, Bootstrap.

Since 2013, Bootstrap has become one of the most popular projects on the code-sharing platform GitHub. It has good community support and a vast ecosystem including templates and extensions built around it. With a modular approach, Bootstrap saves you a considerable amount of time and effort allowing you to focus on the core parts of your web development projects. Released initially by Twitter to maintain consistency in their internal web designing and development projects, Bootstrap has evolved and since the release of Version 3 has been licensed under the open source MIT license.

Mobile-first design

With the advent of mobile phones and tablets, responsive web design is the need of the hour. Earlier, there was the graceful degradation approach wherein you build a website for desktops and then remove features and adapt it for small screen sizes with a lesser set of capabilities resulting in a watered down, subpar browsing experience.

With the release of Bootstrap 3, a mobile-first approach was implemented thereby helping you to create websites that function efficiently on mobile platforms despite the platform constraints. This included taking into account all the restrictions of mobile devices and creating a website that is powerful with cross-browser compatibility giving your website users an awesome mobile experience. Using progressive enhancement techniques, you then add other features for desktop users thereby increasing the accessibility significantly. Thus, your website is well-equipped to handle changes regardless of whether you are using an iPad device, a Windows PC, or any other platform of your choice.

Let's consider that we design a navigation bar for a web page. On a desktop screen, the web page will be displayed as follows:

It is quite evident that the website displays the navbar brand **Packt Publishing** alongside the menu options such as **Books and Videos**, **Articles**, **Categories**, and **Support** with the search field on the right-hand side.

However, on a small screen mobile phone, the web page would be displayed as follows:

On clicking the expandable mobile navigation icon displayed at the top right corner of the mobile screen, the following screen will be displayed:

Thus, you can see the mobile-first approach of Bootstrap demonstrated by the preceding screenshots.

Why Bootstrap

Bootstrap is "batteries-included", meaning that it brings along with it an incredible responsive Grid system and Base CSS, including extensible classes for implementing and enhancing styling for various elements ranging from typography, buttons, tables, forms, and images to mention a few. With an extensive list of components that consist of Glyphicons, responsive navigation bars, BreadCrumbs, Alerts, and much more in addition to official plugins for Modals, Carousels, and PopOvers to name a few, Bootstrap has you covered. With basic knowledge of HTML and CSS, you can understand Bootstrap and implement it in your projects thereby making it a go-to tool for web design.

Let's now look at why Bootstrap is a promising framework for web design:

- **Reusability**: In web designing, a modular pattern is favored as you do not have to rewrite code for various portions of your design. Bootstrap has ready-made components, CSS styles, and plugins that can be included directly in your code. This aspect saves you a considerable amount of time and effort resulting in rapid development. Moreover, this results in easy code maintenance and helps you organize your code efficiently.

- **Consistency**: Easy code readability is crucial for a designer. It also helps that the designers working with you or assigned the same project can understand the code well so as to implement modifications and alterations. As Bootstrap uses ready-made code snippets and is compatible across different browsers, there is a high degree of uniformity in your designing process. This also lowers the learning curve for new designers who want to build on the same project or implement a similar functionality on different projects.

- **Flexible grid layout**: Bootstrap has a default Grid system that can scale up to 12 columns with the relative increase in the screen size and with the flexibility to opt for a fixed or fluid responsive grid. Apart from this, Bootstrap is flexible as you can add any number of customized columns that you may need on a row-by-row basis using its built-in LESS variables and mixins. Using the variables and mixins, you can determine the number of columns and the gutter width as well as the media query point, which decides the threshold for floating columns in addition to generating semantic CSS for individual grid columns. Offsetting and nesting can be implemented easily, with a few lines of code. Using Media Queries and responsive utility classes, you can also manipulate certain blocks of content by making them appear or hide based on the screen size.

- **Customization**: You can customize Bootstrap significantly using the built-in **Customize** option, where you can choose the features that you want to use and uncheck features you don't want, making it as bloat-free as possible. You can use a Custom CSS sheet to override Bootstrap's default styles in addition to using LESS files for CSS preprocessing. Using LESS, you can use variables and mixins to alter almost every defined default attribute. Moreover, you can customize the way plugins such as Modals and Alerts work using advanced JavaScript. As SaaS compatibility and customization were introduced in the latest version of Bootstrap, you can create complex and interactive websites with Bootstrap.

- **Vibrant community with extensive third-party initiatives**: Bootstrap has an active community of developers as well as immense third-party support wherein there is continuous improvisation. Bootlint, an HTML linting tool for projects using Vanilla Bootstrap, was released recently, which helps you identify incorrect Bootstrap usage errors. JavaScript frameworks such as AngularJS are used in conjunction with Bootstrap resulting in the creation of Mobile Angular UI specifically tailored for mobile-based designing. Another recent development is the installation of Bootstrap using the Node package manager. Bootstrap Bay (`http://bootstrapbay.com/`), Bootply (`http://www.bootply.com/`), and Bootsnipp (`http://bootsnipp.com/`) are some of the third-party websites that host a wide range of templates, editors and builders, and tailor-made snippets that help you streamline your web designing using Bootstrap.

- **Futuristic outlook and open development**: The development of Bootstrap is explicitly carried out on GitHub. You can follow all the changes implemented and view the records of outstanding issues with the facility of reporting Bootstrap-related errors and bugs, in addition to contributing to the future development of Bootstrap. The project roadmap can also be found on the official website along with facets such as backward compatibility among the challenges to be addressed in the near future. Bootstrap is a framework that incorporates HTML5 and CSS3 in addition to a plethora of toolsets and utilities thereby shaping up to becoming a benchmark and a vital cog in the wheel for futuristic design and development.

Summary

In this chapter, we had a look at Bootstrap and the reasons to incorporate it in your web designing projects. You understood Bootstrap's mobile-first approach and its relevance in this era where mobiles and tablets are increasingly becoming the first medium for browsing the Web. In the next chapter, we will look at the different ways to install Bootstrap in your projects, which also includes customizing it to build impressive websites.

2
Installing and Customizing Bootstrap

There are several ways to incorporate Bootstrap into your projects. You can customize Bootstrap depending on your requirement and how you intend to utilize it. At times, you need to make minor changes such as adding colors or changing the font size. For these customizations, you need to create your custom CSS and add it after the Bootstrap CSS file. However, there are situations where you may need to make deeper customizations such as using your own semantic CSS classes or elements. In such a scenario, including your own CSS, in addition to the Bootstrap CSS, may be cumbersome due to bloating because of huge file sizes and download time.

In this chapter, we will cover the following ways to use Bootstrap for your projects:

- Including Bootstrap in your project
- The Bootstrap **Content Delivery Network (CDN)**
- Overriding with custom CSS
- The Bootstrap customizer
- Deep customization of Bootstrap
- Compiling LESS files

Including Bootstrap in your HTML file

Download Bootstrap from the official website `http://getbootstrap.com/` and include it in your HTML file with little or no customization.

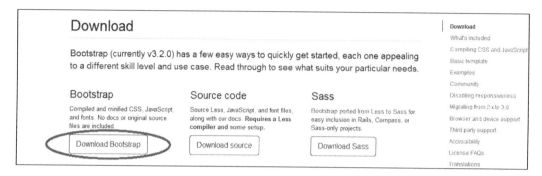

Click on the **Download Bootstrap** button and the file will be downloaded in the ZIP format. The ZIP files contain the Bootstrap CSS, JavaScript, and font files as shown in the following directory structure:

```
bootstrap
|____css
| |____bootstrap.css
| |____bootstrap.min.css
| |____bootstrap.css.map
| |____bootstrap-theme.css
| |____bootstrap-theme.min.css
| |____bootstrap-theme.css.map
|____fonts
| |____glyphiconshalflings-regular.eot
| |____glyphiconshalflings-regular.svg
| |____glyphiconshalflings-regular.ttf
| |____glyphiconshalflings-regular.woff
|____js
| |____bootstrap.js
| |____bootstrap.min.js
```

You need to extract the Bootstrap `.zip` file and copy the contents to your project folder. The next step is to include the CSS and JavaScript files in your HTML file.

Let's take a look at how the file structure should be if you use Bootstrap in your HTML file:

```html
<!DOCTYPE html>
<html>
<head>
<title> Learning Bootstrap with Packt </title>
<meta charset="UTF-8">
<meta name="viewport" content="width=device-width, initial-
scale=1.0">
<!-- Bootstrap -->
<link href="css/bootstrap.min.css" rel="stylesheet"
media="screen">
<link href="css/custom.css" rel="stylesheet" media="screen">
</head>
<body>
<h1> Welcome to Packt </h1>

<!-- JavaScript plugins (requires jQuery) -->
    <script
    src="https://ajax.googleapis.com/ajax/libs/jquery/
    1.11.1/jquery.min.js"></script>
<!-- Include all compiled plugins (below), or include individual
files as needed -->
    <script src="js/bootstrap.min.js"></script>
<!-- Inlcude HTML5 Shim and Respond.js for IE8 support of HTML5
elements and media queries -->
    <script
    src="https://oss.maxcdn.com/html5shiv/3.7.2/html5shiv.min.js">
    </script>
    <script
    src="https://oss.maxcdn.com/respond/1.4.2/respond.min.js">
    </script>
</body>
</html>
```

The output of this code upon execution will be as follows:

Welcome to Packt

Let's discuss the code so that you understand how it all works.

In the preceding code example, in the <head> section, the Bootstrap CSS is linked to the HTML file and then there is a custom CSS file after the Bootstrap CSS, which will help you override the Bootstrap styles. You can also see that we have used the <meta charset="UTF-8"> tag. Whenever the web page is opened locally (from the disk filesystem), the text/html part will instruct the web browser of which type the document is so that it knows how to parse it, and the charset=UTF-8 value will instruct the web browser which character encoding should be used to display the characters on the web page so that it won't use the platform default encoding. After this, we linked the jQuery and JavaScript files in the <body> section. We also added the links for the HTML shiv element along with the respond.js file for IE support and media queries. The respond.js script provides a quick and lightweight script to enable responsive web designs in browsers (specifically Internet Explorer versions 6 to 8), which do not support CSS3 Media Queries.

If you observe the preceding code, you will find that we have used the minified versions, that is, bootstrap.min.js and bootstrap.min.css, to lower the file size resulting in faster loading of the website. You can use the full version in the development stage and the minified version in the production-ready live stage depending on your preference.

The Bootstrap CDN

In the previous code example, you can see that we have used CDN for the HTML5 shiv element and the respond.js file.

A CDN is a large distributed system of servers deployed in multiple data centers across the Internet. Using a CDN means that you save significant bandwidth as the files are not loaded from your server. You can leverage the benefit of a blazing-fast performance, as the files loaded from the CDN are loaded in parallel and not queued by the browser, as they are in a different domain. In addition, the CDN provides data centers closer to the users, meaning that, the server selected is typically based on the user's location and faster routes. Thus, files are loaded faster. In some cases, it abstracts the need to load the files. Plenty of websites use the Bootstrap CDN and if the website users have previously visited one of these websites, then the browser will use that same copy of the Bootstrap files abstracting the need to load Bootstrap again, thereby increasing the performance of your website.

Downloading the example code

You can download the example code files from your account at http://www.packtpub.com for all the Packt Publishing books you have purchased. If you purchased this book elsewhere, you can visit http://www.packtpub.com/support and register to have the files e-mailed directly to you.

The basic structure of the code in the previous example on incorporating the CDN links will look like this:

```
<!DOCTYPE html>
<html>
<head>
<title> Learning Bootstrap with Packt </title>
<meta charset="UTF-8">
<meta name="viewport" content="width=device-width, initial-
scale=1.0">
<!-- The Bootstrap minified CDN CSS Link -->
<link rel="stylesheet"
href="//maxcdn.bootstrapcdn.com/bootstrap/3.2.0/css/bootstrap.min.
css">
<link href="css/custom.css" rel="stylesheet" media="screen">
</head>
<body>
<h1> Welcome to Packt </h1>
<!-- JavaScript plugins (requires jQuery) -->
<script
src="https://ajax.googleapis.com/ajax/libs/jquery/1.11.1/jquery.
min.js"></script>
<!-- The Bootstrap minified JavaScript CDN link -->
<script
src="//maxcdn.bootstrapcdn.com/bootstrap/3.2.0/js/bootstrap.min.
js"></script>
<!-- Include HTML5 Shim and Respond.js for IE6-8 support of HTML5
elements and media queries -->
<script
src="https://oss.maxcdn.com/html5shiv/3.7.2/html5shiv.min.js">
</script>
<script src="https://oss.maxcdn.com/respond/1.4.2/respond.min.js">
</script>
</body>
</html>
```

You must be online if you are using CDN. If you are offline, then you have to use the Bootstrap CSS and JavaScript files available in the downloaded ZIP file. Download the compressed or uncompressed jQuery JavaScript file from this link for offline use http://jquery.com/download/.

Also, you need to download the `respond.js` file from the GitHub site and include it in your project. The link for the `respond.js` file is `https://github.com/scottjehl/Respond`.

Click on the highlighted **Download ZIP** button as shown in the following screenshot:

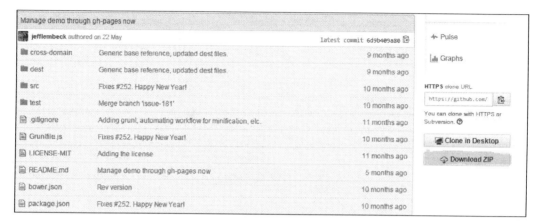

Extract the `respond.js` zip file. On unzipping the file, you need to go to the `dest` folder and copy the `respond.min` JavaScript file. You need to include this file in the JavaScript folder. However, as a website functions online, it is a good practice to use CDN for your web projects.

 In this book, we will use CDN in a few of the chapters as you should not be confused with all the code ingrained in the HTML document. For clarity and to prevent information overload, we will stick to the CDN methodology.

Overriding with custom CSS

The easiest way to customize Bootstrap is to create your custom CSS file where you will put your own CSS code. The link to this customized CSS file needs to be added after the Bootstrap CSS in your HTML document for it to override the Bootstrap CSS declarations.

Look at the following code to understand it better:

```
<!DOCTYPE html>
<html>
<head>
<title>BootStrap with Packt</title>
```

```
<meta charset="UTF-8">
<meta name="viewport" content="width=device-width, initial-
scale=1.0">
<!-- Latest Bootstrap CDN CSS -->
<link rel="stylesheet"
href="https://maxcdn.bootstrapcdn.com/bootstrap/3.2.0/css/
bootstrap.min.css">
</head>
<body>
<h1>Welcome to Packt</h1>
<button type="button" class="btn btn-default btn-sm"
id="packt">PACKT LESSONS</button>
<!-- Latest compiled and minified JavaScript -->
<script
src="https://maxcdn.bootstrapcdn.com/bootstrap/3.2.0/js/bootstrap.
min.js"></script>
</body>
</html>
```

In the preceding code example, we did not include the external style sheet. The output of the code on execution will be as follows:

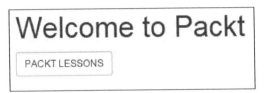

Consider the same preceding HTML code. Let's link it to an external style sheet custom.css. On adding the link, the code will look like this:

```
<!DOCTYPE html>
<html>
<head>
<title>BootStrap with Packt</title>
<meta charset="UTF-8">
<meta name="viewport" content="width=device-width, initial-
scale=1.0">
<!-- Latest Bootstrap CDN CSS -->
<link rel="stylesheet"
href="https://maxcdn.bootstrapcdn.com/bootstrap/3.2.0/css/
bootstrap.min.css">
<link href="custom.css" rel="stylesheet" media="screen">
</head>
<body>
```

```
<h1>Welcome to Packt</h1>
<button type="button" class="btn btn-default btn-sm"
id="packt">PACKT LESSONS</button>
<!-- Latest compiled and minified JavaScript -->
<script
src="https://maxcdn.bootstrapcdn.com/bootstrap/3.2.0/js/bootstrap.
min.js"></script>
</body>
</html>
```

 The CSS file should be in the same folder as the HTML document. If not, then you need to specify the location of the style sheet.

We will now write the code for the custom.css file:

```
#packt    {
   padding: 19px 30px;
      -webkit-border-radius: 35px;
      -moz-border-radius: 35px;
   border-radius: 35px;
   color: red
}
```

Once we save this custom.css file, the output of the code will be as follows:

As you can see, the **PACKT LESSONS** button that was referenced by the packt ID will be displayed differently according to the border-radius padding and the red color assigned to it.

 Placing all your customizations in your own CSS files instead of modifying the Bootstrap files is a good practice. This approach helps you, particularly when a new version comes along and you are upgrading Bootstrap, as all you need to do is replace the Bootstrap files in your project folder by the latest ones (provided the newer versions in the future support backward compatibility).

Using the Bootstrap customizer

In some cases, you might want to use a small subset of features included in Bootstrap. In such scenarios, you can use the Bootstrap customizer. Click on the **Customize** icon on the official Bootstrap website.

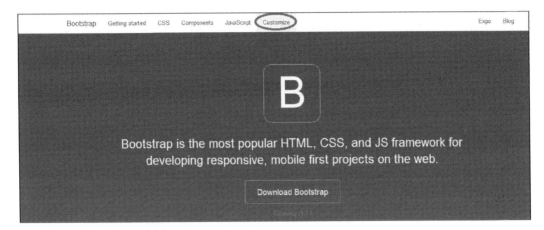

Once you click on **Customize**, you will see the following screen:

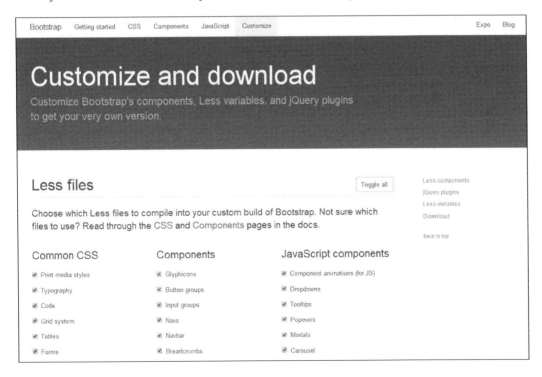

Uncheck the features you do not need for your projects. Then you can click on the **Compile and Download** button.

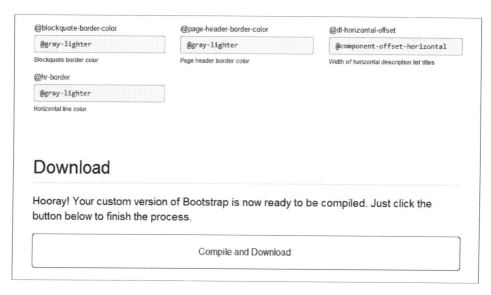

On clicking the button, you will get a ZIP file with the same directory structure as the regular download but the file size will be lower depending on the features you chose for your projects. Thus, you can leverage the benefit of faster performance and quick website loading, as you are only loading the specific features instead of the complete bundle.

 You need to remember the customization and go through the same procedure if you want to upgrade to the latest version in the future.

Deep customization of Bootstrap

Adding your own style sheet works when you are trying to do something quick or when the modifications are minimal. Customizing Bootstrap beyond small changes involves using the uncompiled Bootstrap source code. The Bootstrap CSS source code is written in LESS with **variables** and **mixins** to allow easy customization.

 LESS is an open source CSS preprocessor with cool features used to speed up your development time. LESS allows you to engage an efficient and modular style of working making it easier to maintain your CSS styling in your projects.

The advantages of using variables in LESS are profound. You can reuse the same code many times thereby following the write once, use anywhere paradigm. Variables can be globally declared, which allows you to specify certain values in a single place. This needs to be updated only once if changes are required.

LESS variables allow you to specify widely used values such as colors, font family, and sizes in a single file. By modifying a single variable, the changes will be reflected in all the Bootstrap components that use it; for example, to change the background color of the body element to green (#00FF00 is the hexadecimal code for green), all you need to do is change the value of the variable called @body-bg in Bootstrap as shown in the following code:

```
@body-bg: #00FF00;
```

Mixins are similar to variables but for whole classes. Mixins enable you to embed the properties of a class into another. It allows you to group multiple code lines together so that it can be used numerous times across the style sheet. Mixins can also be used alongside variables and functions resulting in multiple inheritances; for example, to add clearfix to an article, you can use the .clearfix mixin as shown in the left column of the following table. It will result in all clearfix declarations included in the compiled CSS code shown in the right column:

<pre>article
{
  .clearfix;
}</pre>
	<pre>{
	article:before,
	article:after
	{
	content: " "; // 1
	display: table; // 2
	}
	article:after
	{
	    clear: both;
	}
	}</pre>

A clearfix mixin is a way for an element to automatically clear after itself, so that you don't need to add additional markup. It's generally used in float layouts, where elements are floated to be stacked horizontally.

Downloading the Bootstrap source code

You can download the Bootstrap source code package containing the LESS files and other components if you want to customize Bootstrap beyond small modifications. There are several ways to obtain the source code. The easiest way to obtain the source code is from the official website at `http://getbootstrap.com/getting-started/#download`. Refer to the following screenshot for the highlighted button for the source code:

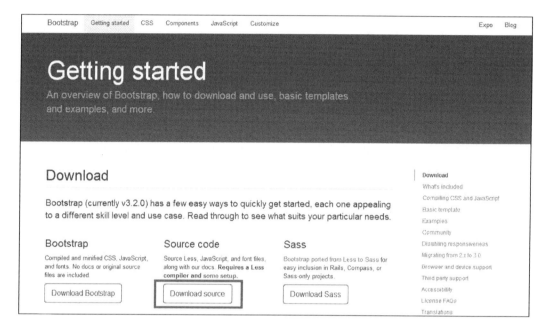

Once you click on the **Download source** button, you will obtain the source code package in a ZIP format. On unzipping, we get the following screen wherein you can view the `less` folder, various other tools such as the `grunt` task runner, and other source code elements:

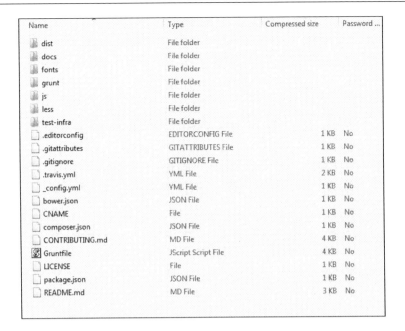

Alternatively, you can find the entire source code on GitHub at `https://github.com/twbs/bootstrap`. On the same page, click on the highlighted link shown clearly in the following screenshot to obtain the source code in the ZIP format:

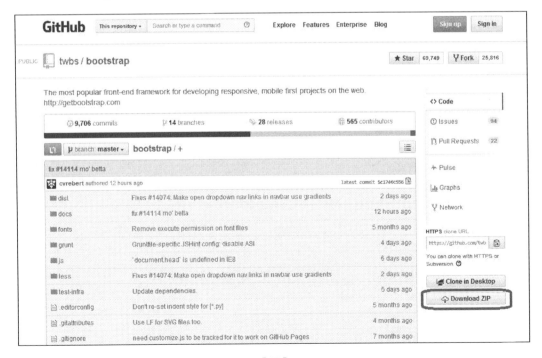

On unzipping it, you will see the source code, which is similar to the one downloaded from the official website. Unzip the package and you will find all the components, LESS files, and other folders.

> You can also use the Bower web package manager available at `http://bower.io/`. Run the command `bower install bootstrap` in your project folder to download Bootstrap.

Compiling LESS files

You can compile your Bootstrap file using two different methods. Either you can use a GUI program such as SimpLESS or WinLess to compile your LESS files or use the command line as per your preference.

Using SimpLESS to compile LESS files

SimpLESS is a product developed by KISS, an organization based in Germany. You can download SimpLESS from the official website at `http://wearekiss.com/simpless`. It is a multi-platform tool, meaning it works well on Windows, Mac, and Linux.

After installing SimpLESS, you will see the interface as depicted in the following screenshot:

You need to drag-and-drop the `bootstrap.less` file from the `less` folder to SimpLESS. SimpLESS includes on the fly compilation, meaning that it will automatically compile to `bootstrap.css` every time you modify and save the LESS files. It comes with power-packed features such as minification, out-of-the-box notifications, and an automatic LESS updater.

Using WinLess to compile LESS files

WinLess is a GUI for the Windows platform to convert LESS to CSS. You can download the WinLess utility from the official website at `http://winless.org/`.

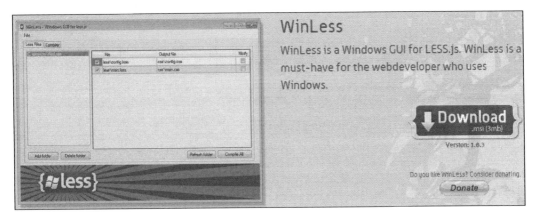

Once you download the utility, you need to click on the installer and click on **Run**. You can launch the utility and you will see the following screen:

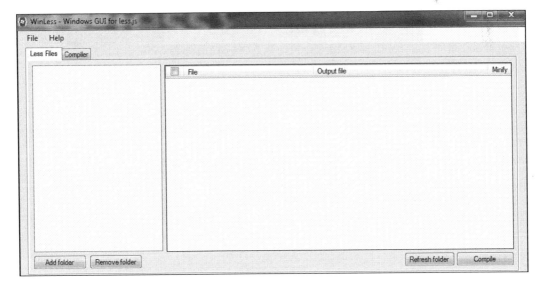

You can either add the folder containing LESS files or drop the required folder in the folder pane. Click on **Compile** and the conversion from LESS to CSS takes place. You just need to click on **Refresh folder** for the changes to reflect in your folder.

We will use the WinLess utility to convert the LESS files to CSS in this chapter.

Using the command line to compile LESS files

You can also compile LESS using the command line via the NPM, which is the Node package manager. NPM is installed simultaneously when you install Node.js on your computer. You can download the latest version of Node.js from the official Node.js website at http://nodejs.org/download/.

Run the following command to install LESS:

```
npm install -g less
```

Once LESS is installed, you can use it from the following command line:

```
lessc bootstrap.less > bootstrap.css
```

To generate a minified version of the CSS file, add the --yui-compress option to the previous command:

```
lessc --yui-compress bootstrap.less > bootstrap.min.css
```

If you want the file to be automatically compiled when you make a change, you can also use the watch option, -w.

Putting it all together

Until now, we have discussed the various aspects of Bootstrap with LESS. We are not using the Bootstrap CSS CDN in this example as we are going to alter the bootstrap.less file, which will compile to bootstrap.css using the WinLess compiler.

You will now implement the knowledge you gained in a step-by-step approach:

1. Download and unzip the Bootstrap files into a folder.
2. Create an HTML file called bootstrap_example and save it in the same folder where you saved the Bootstrap files.

The code for the `bootstrap_example` HTML document is as follows:

```
<!DOCTYPE html>
<html>
<head>
<title>BootStrap with Packt</title>
<meta charset="UTF-8">
<meta name="viewport" content="width=device-width, initial-
scale=1.0">
<!-- Downloaded Bootstrap CSS -->
<link href="css/bootstrap.css" rel="stylesheet">
<!-- JavaScript plugins (requires jQuery) -->
<script
src="https://ajax.googleapis.com/ajax/libs/jquery/1.11.1/
jquery.min.js"></script>
<!-- Include all compiled plugins (below), or include individual
files as needed -->
<script src="js/bootstrap.min.js"></script>
</head>
<body>
<h1>Welcome to Packt</h1>
<button type="button" class="btn btn-default btn-lg"
id="packt">PACKT LESSONS</button>
</body>
</html>
```

The output of this code upon execution will be as follows:

3. The Bootstrap folder includes the following folders and file:

   ○   css

   ○   fonts

   ○   js

   ○   bootstrap_example.html

This Bootstrap folder is shown in the following screenshot:

4. Since we are going to use the Bootstrap source code now, let's download the ZIP file and keep it at any location. Unzip it and we can see the contents of the folder as shown in the following screenshot:

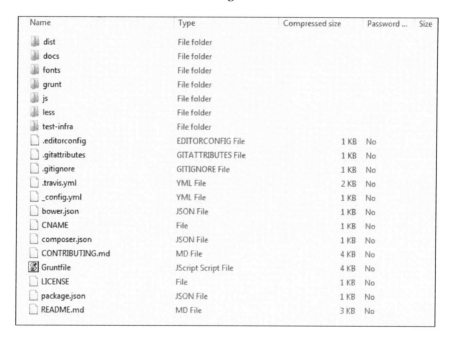

5. Let's now create a new folder called `bootstrap` in the `css` folder. The contents of our `css` folder will appear as displayed in the following screenshot:

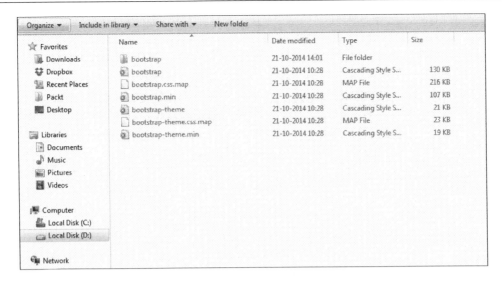

6. Copy the contents of the `less` folder from the source code and paste it into the newly created `bootstrap` folder inside the `css` folder. Thus, contents of the same `bootstrap` folder within the `css` folder will appear as displayed in the following screenshot:

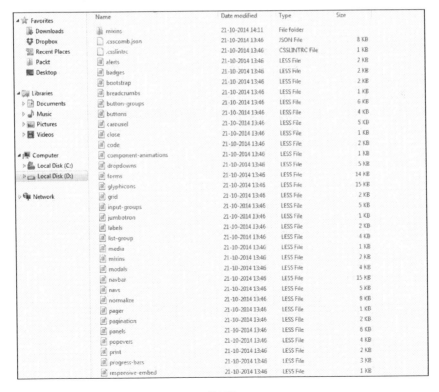

7. In the `bootstrap` folder, look for the `variable.less` file and open it using Notepad or Notepad++. In this example, we are using a simple Notepad and on opening the `variable.less` file with Notepad, we can see the contents of the file as shown in the following screenshot:

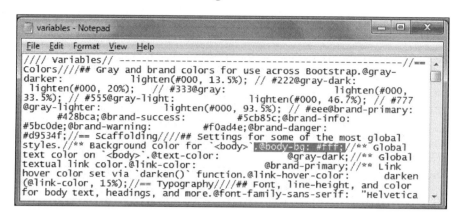

8. Currently, we can see `@body-bg` is assigned the default value `#fff` as the color code. Change the background color of the body element to green by assigning the value `#00ff00` to it. Save the file and later on, look for the `bootstrap.less` file in the `bootstrap` folder. In the next step, we are going to use WinLess.

9. Open WinLess and add the contents of the `bootstrap` folder to it. In the folder pane, you will see all the `less` files loaded as shown in the following screenshot:

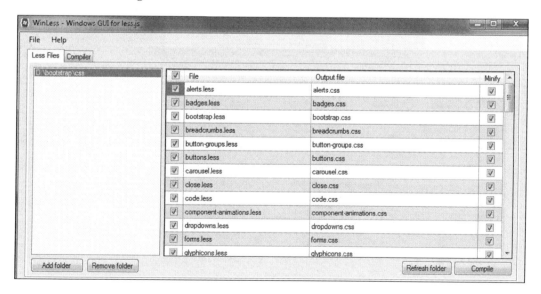

10. Now we need to uncheck all the files and only select the `bootstrap.less` file as shown in following screenshot:

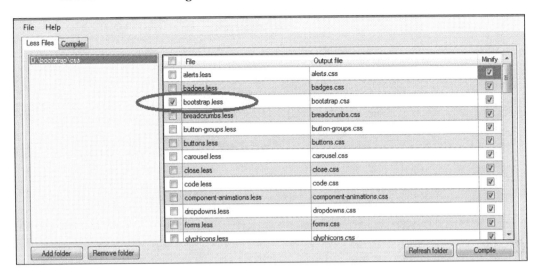

11. Click on **Compile**. This will compile your `bootstrap.less` file to `bootstrap.css`. Copy the newly compiled `bootstrap.css` file from the `bootstrap` folder and paste it into the `css` folder thereby replacing the original `bootstrap.css` file.

12. Now that we have the updated `bootstrap.css` file, go back to `bootstrap_example.html` and execute it. Upon execution, the output of the code would be as follows:

Thus, we can see that the background color of the `<body>` element turns to green as we have altered it globally in the `variables.less` file that was linked to the `bootstrap.less` file, which was later compiled to `bootstrap.css` by WinLess.

We can also use LESS variables and mixins to customize Bootstrap. We can import the Bootstrap files and add our customizations:

13. Let's now create our own less file called `styles.less` in the `css` folder. We will now include the Bootstrap files by adding the following line of code in the `styles.less` file:

```
@import "./bootstrap/bootstrap.less";
```

 We have given the path `./bootstrap/bootstrap.less` as per the location of the `bootstrap.less` file. Remember to give the exact path if you have placed it at any other location.

14. Now, let's try a few customizations and add the following code to `styles.less`:

```
@body-bg: #FFA500;
@padding-large-horizontal: 40px;
@font-size-base: 7px;
@line-height-base: 9px;
@border-radius-large: 75px;
```

15. The next step is to compile the `styles.less` file to `styles.css`. We will again use WinLess for this purpose. You have to uncheck all options and select only `styles.less` to be compiled.

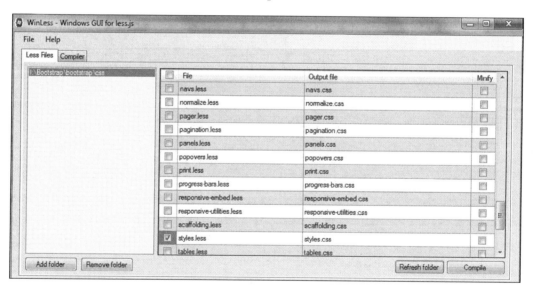

16. On compilation, the `styles.css` file will contain all the CSS declarations from Bootstrap. The next step would be to add the `styles.css` style sheet to the `bootstrap_example.html` file.

So your HTML code will look like this:

```html
<!DOCTYPE html>
<html>
<head>
<title>BootStrap with Packt</title>
<meta charset="UTF-8">
<meta name="viewport" content="width=device-width, initial-scale=1.0">
<!-- Downloaded Bootstrap CSS -->
<link href="css/bootstrap.css" rel="stylesheet">
<!-- JavaScript plugins (requires jQuery) -->
<script
src="https://ajax.googleapis.com/ajax/libs/jquery/1.11.1/
jquery.min.js"></script>
<!-- Include all compiled plugins (below), or include individual
files as needed -->
<script src="js/bootstrap.min.js"></script>
<link href="css/styles.css" rel="stylesheet">
</head>
<body>
<h1>Welcome to Packt</h1>
<button type="button" class="btn btn-default btn-lg"
id="packt">PACKT LESSONS</button>
</body>
</html>
```

The output of the code is as follows:

Since we changed the background color to orange (`#ffa500`), created a border radius, and defined `font-size-base` and `line-height-base`, the output that was displayed in the preceding screenshot changed.

The LESS variables should be added to the `styles.less` file after the Bootstrap import so that they override the variables defined in the Bootstrap files. In short, all the custom code you write should be added after the Bootstrap import.

Summary

In this chapter, you understood the different ways to incorporate Bootstrap into your projects. You also reviewed the ways in which you can customize Bootstrap to suit your web designing requirements. From including Bootstrap in your projects, implementing simple customizations to deep customization involving compiling LESS variables, we have covered the entire concept of installation and customizations in a practical manner.

In the next chapter, you will learn about the Bootstrap Grid and how to use it in your projects.

3
Using the Bootstrap Grid

Grids help you achieve consistency in your designs by offering you a structure to put your design elements in. Prior to Bootstrap 3, you had to add mobile styles explicitly. Bootstrap 3 has changed all that by adapting a mobile-first approach with mobile styles baked-in to the core. All the columns are stacked on small mobile phone screens, with the grid scaling up to 12 columns on the large screen. The Grid system in Bootstrap helps you add CSS classes to block elements such as `<div>` in your HTML documents.

The new Bootstrap Grid system adapts a mobile-first approach, and therefore, when you declare a specific grid size, it becomes the grid for that size and higher. In other words, if you define a size at `sm` (small-screen-sized devices), then it will be that grid size for `sm`, `md` (medium-screen-sized devices), and `lg` (large-screen-sized devices). We will get to this later in the chapter, so please do not get overwhelmed with the overload of description at this stage.

Alternatively, you can use LESS variables and mixins for greater customization and flexibility. In Bootstrap 3, you use `Normalize.css` for cross-browser rendering.

 The `Normalize.css` file makes browsers render all elements more consistently and in line with modern standards. It precisely targets only the styles that need normalizing.

In this chapter, we will cover the following topics:

- Using the Bootstrap Grid classes
- Adding rows and columns
- Adding offsets to columns
- Reversing the order of columns

- Nesting columns
- Using the Bootstrap variables and mixins
- Creating a blog layout with the Bootstrap Grid mixins and variables

Using the Bootstrap Grid classes

You can create a page layout through a series of rows and columns that house your content. To set the maximum width of the page content according to the screen width, you have to use the .container class.

 Containers help define the space to be used by the Grid system.

The container width is set as follows:

- Phone screens (less than 768 px resolution): The width of the container is the same width as the width of the screen
- Tablet screens (between 768 px and 992 px resolution): The maximum width of the container is 750 px
- Small desktop screens (between 992 px and 1200 px resolution): The maximum width of the container is 970 px
- Large desktop screens (more than 1200 px resolution): The maximum width of the container is 1170 px

The class prefixes used for small phone screens, tablets, small desktop screens, and large desktop screens are .col-xs-, .col-sm-, .col-md-, and .col-lg-, respectively. The default gutter width is 30 px.

 Gutters are usually desirable because the white space between columns makes for better legibility, so it makes sense to include them as part of the automation for the layout. As for Bootstrap, the gutter width of 30 px is ingrained in it.

While the column width for small devices is automatic, the column widths for tablets, small desktops, and large screens are 62 px, 81 px, and 97 px, respectively.

In order to understand this better, take a look at the following code:

```
<!DOCTYPE html>
<html>
  <head>
    <title>Using the Bootstrap Grid classes</title>
    <meta name="viewport" content="width=device-width, initial-
    scale=1.0">
    <!-- Bootstrap -->
    <link href="css/bootstrap.min.css" rel="stylesheet"
    media="screen">
  </head>
  <body>
    <div class="container">
    </div>
  </body>
</html>
```

The `<!DOCTYPE html>` doctype is used so that HTML5 tags are properly displayed by the browsers. The `viewport` meta tag is used to make mobile devices display the page responsively instead of trying to display them at desktop sizes. The `<div>` tag referenced by the container class will contain the page content. The `container` class is for a responsive fixed width container, whereas for a full width container spanning the entire width of the viewport, we use the `container-fluid` class.

Adding rows and columns

You can create rows and columns on the page using the row and column CSS classes. You have to use rows to create a horizontal group of columns, and only columns can be immediate children of rows. Usually, you can use the `.col-md-` Grid classes to develop a system that is displayed as stacked in small devices; they turn horizontal on the desktop and large screens. The `col` class should be used in conjunction with the `.col-md-X` class (where X is the grid unit width that the block element should have) to add a width to the columns. The total number of columns in a row should not be greater than 12, which is the default for the maximum number of columns in a single row on desktops and large screens.

Take a look at the following code to understand this better:

```html
<!DOCTYPE html>
<html>
  <head>
    <title>Using the Bootstrap Grid classes</title>
    <meta name="viewport" content="width=device-width, initial-
    scale=1.0">
    <!-- Bootstrap -->
    <link href="css/bootstrap.min.css" rel="stylesheet"
    media="screen">
  </head>
  <body>
    <div class="container">
      <h1> Welcome to Packt Publishing </h1>
      <p>An example to showcase the Bootstrap Grid
      classes</p>

      <div class="row">
        <div class="col-md-4">
          <h2>PacktPub</h2>
            <p>Packt is one of the most prolific and fast-
              growing tech book publishers in the world.
              Originally focused on open source software, Packt
              pays a royalty on relevant books directly to open
              source projects. These projects have received over
              $400,000 as part of Packt's Open Source Royalty
              Scheme to date.
          </p>
        </div>
        <div class="col-md-4">
          <h2>PacktLib: The Packt Online Library</h2>
          <p>
            PacktLib is Packt's online digital book library.
            Launched in August 2010, it allows you to access and
            search almost 100,000 pages of book content, to find
            the solutions you need.
          </p>
        </div>
        <div class="col-md-4">
          <h2>Work for Packt Birmingham</h2>
          <p>
            Packt Publishing is a young, ground-breaking computer
            book publishing company with a large and fast-growing
            online customer base. With a highly ranked website and
            innovating constantly into new business areas, we are
```

```
       at the cutting-edge of digital publishing, web
       marketing and e-commerce development. Our unique
       strategy of publishing highly-focused and practical
       technical books on new and ground-breaking
       technologies has driven rapid growth and we are now
       poised for expansion. This can be seen from our recent
       move to new offices in the heart of Birmingham.
     </p>
    </div>
   </div>
  </div>
 </body>
</html>
```

The output of the code upon the execution will be as follows:

Welcome to Packt Publishing

An example to showcase the Bootstrap Grid classes

PacktPub

Packt is one of the most prolific and fast-growing tech book publishers in the world. Originally focused on open source software, Packt pays a royalty on relevant books directly to open source projects. These projects have received over $400,000 as part of Packt's Open Source Royalty Scheme to date

PacktLib: The Packt Online Library

PacktLib is Packt's online digital book library. Launched in August 2010, it allows you to access and search almost 100,000 pages of book content, to find the solutions you need.

Work for Packt Birmingham

Packt Publishing is a young, ground-breaking computer book publishing company with a large and fast-growing online customer base. With a highly ranked website and innovating constantly into new business areas, we are at the cutting-edge of digital publishing, web marketing and e-commerce development. Our unique strategy of publishing highly-focused and practical technical books on new and ground-breaking technologies has driven rapid growth and we are now poised for expansion. This can be seen from our recent move to new offices in the heart of Birmingham.

If you observe the code and the output, you will see a grid with three columns, each with a width of 4. If you observe the `<h1>` and `<p>` tags, you will see that they have been declared before the row was defined. However, the three columns with the **PacktPub**, **PacktLib: The Packt Online Library** and **Work for Packt Birmingham** headings have been defined with a width of 4 per column. Thus, the 12 columns get divided into three parts with a width of 4 each. However, this format will only define the layout on the desktop or a large screen. The entire grid will be stacked in small devices and will be horizontally aligned on a desktop or a large screen.

If you want the content to span the full width of the container, you don't have to define it between a row or a column, meaning the CSS class `col-md-12` to create full width columns is not mandatory. Also, if you have more than 12 columns in a single row, the extra columns will get wrapped as a unit on the next line.

Customizing the grid for small devices

As already mentioned, columns will be displayed one after the other on a small screen. Suppose that you want a column-based format for small devices as well. In such a scenario, you have to include the `col-sm-x` CSS class in the code.

Take a look at the following code to understand it better:

```
<!DOCTYPE html>
<html>
  <head>
    <title>Using the Bootstrap Grid classes</title>
    <meta name="viewport" content="width=device-width, initial-
    scale=1.0">
    <!-- Bootstrap -->
    <link href="css/bootstrap.min.css" rel="stylesheet"
    media="screen">
  </head>
  <body>
    <div class="container">
      <h1> Welcome to Packt Publishing </h1>
      <p>An example to showcase the Bootstrap Grid classes</p>

      <div class="row">
        <div class="col-md-4 col-sm-6">
          <h2>PacktPub</h2>
          <p>Packt is one of the most prolific and fast-growing
            tech book publishers in the world. Originally focused
            on open source software, Packt pays a royalty on
            relevant books directly to open source projects. These
            projects have received over $400,000 as part of
            Packt's Open Source Royalty Scheme to date.</p>
        </div>
        <div class="col-md-4 col-sm-6">
          <h2>PacktLib: Online </h2>
          <p>
            PacktLib is Packt's online digital book library.
            Launched in August 2010, it allows you to access and
            search almost 100,000 pages of book content, to find
            the solutions you need.
          </p>
```

```
      </div>
      <div class="col-md-4 col-sm-12">
        <h2>Packt Birmingham</h2>
        <p>
          Packt Publishing is a young, ground-breaking computer
          book publishing company with a large and fast-growing
          online customer base. With a highly ranked website and
          innovating constantly into new business areas, we are
          at the cutting-edge of digital publishing, web
          marketing and e-commerce development. Our unique
          strategy of publishing highly-focused and practical
          technical books on new and ground-breaking
          technologies has driven rapid growth and we are now
          poised for expansion. This can be seen from our recent
          move to new offices in the heart of Birmingham.
        </p>
      </div>
    </div>
  </div>
</body>
</html>
```

The output of the code on the desktop and large screens upon execution will be as follows:

Welcome to Packt Publishing

An example to showcase the Bootstrap Grid classes

PacktPub

Packt is one of the most prolific and fast-growing tech book publishers in the world. Originally focused on open source software, Packt pays a royalty on relevant books directly to open source projects. These projects have received over $400,000 as part of Packt's Open Source Royalty Scheme to date.

PacktLib: Online

PacktLib is Packt's online digital book library. Launched in August 2010, it allows you to access and search almost 100,000 pages of book content, to find the solutions you need.

Packt Birmingham

Packt Publishing is a young, ground-breaking computer book publishing company with a large and fast-growing online customer base. With a highly ranked website and innovating constantly into new business areas, we are at the cutting-edge of digital publishing, web marketing and e-commerce development. Our unique strategy of publishing highly-focused and practical technical books on new and ground-breaking technologies has driven rapid growth and we are now poised for expansion. This can be seen from our recent move to new offices in the heart of Birmingham.

On a small screen such as a mobile phone or tablet, the output will be as follows:

Welcome to Packt Publishing

An example to showcase the Bootstrap Grid classes

PacktPub

Packt is one of the most prolific and fast-growing tech book publishers in the world. Originally focused on open source software, Packt pays a royalty on relevant books directly to open source projects. These projects have received over $400,000 as part of Packt's Open Source Royalty Scheme to date.

PacktLib: Online

PacktLib is Packt's online digital book library. Launched in August 2010, it allows you to access and search almost 100,000 pages of book content, to find the solutions you need.

Packt Birmingham

Packt Publishing is a young, ground-breaking computer book publishing company with a large and fast-growing online customer base. With a highly ranked website and innovating constantly into new business areas, we are at the cutting-edge of digital publishing, web marketing and e-commerce development. Our unique strategy of publishing highly-focused and practical technical books on new and ground-breaking technologies has driven rapid growth and we are now poised for expansion. This can be seen from our recent move to new offices in the heart of Birmingham.

If you observe the output of the code on a small screen, you can see that since the first two columns were assigned the col-sm-6 class, each of them occupied half the screen width. The third column, which was assigned the col-sm-12 class, occupies the entire screen width below the first two columns.

Adding offsets to columns

In order to add a left margin to columns, you can use the col-offset-X class, where X is the number of columns by which a block element should be moved to the right.

Take a look at the following code to understand this better:

```
<!DOCTYPE html>
<html>
  <head>
    <title>Using the Bootstrap Grid classes</title>
    <meta name="viewport" content="width=device-width, initial-scale=1.0">
    <!-- Bootstrap -->
```

```
    <link href="css/bootstrap.min.css" rel="stylesheet"
    media="screen">
  </head>
  <body>
    <div class="container">
      <h1>The Offset feature in Bootstrap</h1>
      <h2>PacktPub</h2>
      <div class="row">
        <div class="col-md-4 col-md-offset-8">Packt is one of the
        most prolific and fast-growing tech book publishers in the
        world. Originally focused on open source software, Packt
        pays a royalty on relevant books directly to open source
        projects. These projects have received over $400,000 as
        part of Packt's Open Source Royalty Scheme to date.
        </div>
      </div>
    </div>
  </body>
</html>
```

The output of the code upon the execution will be as follows:

The Offset feature in Bootstrap

PacktPub

Packt is one of the most prolific and fast-growing tech book publishers in the world. Originally focused on open source software, Packt pays a royalty on relevant books directly to open source projects. These projects have received over $400,000 as part of Packt's Open Source Royalty Scheme to date.

If you observe the code and the output, you can see that the block element has moved eight column units to the right. If you look at the highlighted code, which is `<div class="col-md-4 col-md-offset-8">`, you can see that we have defined the offset as 8, due to which we get the desired output wherein the `.col-md-offset-8` class will be applied to medium device screen resolutions.

 You can add independent offsets based on the mobile device screen resolution.

Pulling and pushing columns

At times, you might want to display the columns on the screen in a different order than the way in which they are defined in the HTML code. Bootstrap provides the col-push-X and col-pull-X classes for this. While col-push-X will move the column to the right by X units, col-pull-x will move the column to the left by X units, where X is the number of units by which you want to move the columns. This feature helps you reverse the order of columns.

Take a look at the following code to understand this better:

```
<!DOCTYPE html>
<html>
  <head>
    <title>Using the Bootstrap Grid classes</title>
    <meta name="viewport" content="width=device-width, initial-
    scale=1.0">
    <!-- Bootstrap -->
    <link href="css/bootstrap.min.css" rel="stylesheet"
    media="screen">
  </head>
  <body>
    <div class="container">
      <h1>Welcome to Packt</h1>
      <p>We will look at the concept of Grid Layouts now</p>
      <div class="row">
        <div class="col-md-9 col-md-push-3">
          <h2>PacktPub</h2>
          <p>
            Packt is one of the most prolific and fast-growing
            tech book publishers in the world. Originally focused
            on open source software, Packt pays a royalty on
            relevant books directly to open source projects. These
            projects have received over $400,000 as part of
            Packt's Open Source Royalty Scheme to date.Our books
            focus on practicality, recognising that readers are
            ultimately concerned with getting the job done.
            Packt's digitally-focused business model allows us to
            publish up-to-date books in very specific areas.
          </p>
        </div>
        <div class="col-md-3 col-md-pull-9">
          <h2>PacktLib: Online</h2>
          <p>PacktLib is Packt's online digital book library.
            Launched in August 2010, it allows you to access and
            search almost 100,000 pages of book content, to find
            the solutions you need.</p>
```

```
            </div>
          </div>
        </div>
      </body>
    </html>
```

The output of the code upon the execution will be as follows:

Welcome to Packt

We will look at the concept of Grid Layouts now

PacktLib: Online

PacktLib is Packt's online digital book library. Launched in August 2010, it allows you to access and search almost 100,000 pages of book content, to find the solutions you need.

PacktPub

Packt is one of the most prolific and fast-growing tech book publishers in the world. Originally focused on open source software, Packt pays a royalty on relevant books directly to open source projects. These projects have received over $400,000 as part of Packt's Open Source Royalty Scheme to date. Our books focus on practicality, recognising that readers are ultimately concerned with getting the job done. Packt's digitally-focused business model allows us to publish up-to-date books in very specific areas

If you take a look at the preceding code and output, you'll realize that the column with a width of 9 units was pushed to the right by 3 units, whereas the column with a width of 3 units was moved to the left by 9 units. Thus, you can change the output using the `push` and `pull` attributes that override the hierarchy of the HTML code.

Nesting columns

You can nest columns by putting rows and columns within an existing column. The nested columns collectively take the width of the existing parent column.

Take a look at the following code to understand this better:

```
<!DOCTYPE html>
<html>
  <head>
    <title>Using the Bootstrap Grid classes</title>
    <meta name="viewport" content="width=device-width, initial-
    scale=1.0">
    <!-- Bootstrap -->
    <link href="css/bootstrap.min.css" rel="stylesheet"
    media="screen">
    <style>
      #packt {
        border-style: solid;
        border-color: black;
        color: #FF00FF;
      }
      #pub {
```

```
      border-style: solid;
      border-color: black;
      color: #FF00FF;
    }

  #packtlib {
      border-style: dotted;
      border-color: lime;


    }
  </style>

</head>
<body>
  <div class="container">
    <h1>Hello, world!</h1>
    <p>This is an example to show how to nest columns within the
    allocated parent space</p>

    <div class="row ">
      <div class="col-lg-6" id="packtlib">
        <h2>Columns can be nested within the space.</h2>
        <div class="row"   >
          <div class="col-lg-6" id="packt">
            <p>PacktLib is Packt's online digital book library.
              Launched in August 2010, it allows you to access
              and search almost 100,000 pages of book content,
              to find the solutions you need. As part of the
              Open Source community, Packt aims to help sustain
              the projects which it publishes books on. Open
              Source projects have received over $400,000
              through this scheme to date.
            </p>
          </div>
          <div class="col-lg-6" id="pub">
            <p>Our books focus on practicality, recognising that
              readers are ultimately concerned with getting the
              job done. Packt's digitally-focused business model
              allows us to publish up-to-date books in very
              specific areas.With over 1000 books published,
              Packt now offers a subscription service. This app
              and a PacktLib subscription now makes finding the
              information you need easier than ever before.
            </p>
```

```
            </div>
          </div>
        </div>
      </div> <!-- the row class div -->
    </div> <!-- the container div -->
  </body>
</html>
```

The output of the code upon the execution will be as follows:

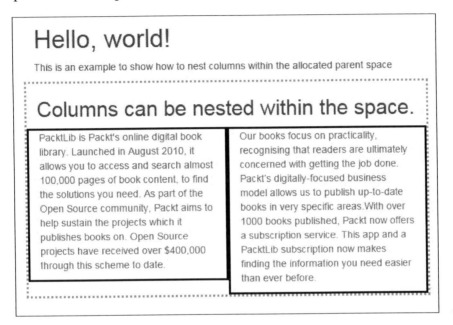

If you take a look at the preceding code and the subsequent output, you can see that we have nested two columns with the `col-lg-6` class within an existing parent column, which has also been assigned a class of `col-lg-6`. The parent column occupies half of the screen width on a desktop or a large screen. The nested columns—each of which has been assigned a `col-lg-6` class—will take half the width of the parent column. You can also see the CSS styles (defined in the `<style>` tag) being applied to the borders of the parent and nested columns. The parent column has a dotted lime-colored border, whereas the child columns nested in the parent column have been assigned a solid black border. From the borders, you can clearly see that the child columns have occupied half the width of the parent column.

Using the Bootstrap variables and mixins

You can use variables and mixins in Bootstrap to build semantic layouts. We will now look at variables used in Bootstrap for the grid layout.

Bootstrap comes with built-in variables and mixins for building semantic grid layouts.

Bootstrap Grid variables

The LESS code for the Bootstrap Grid contains three variables:

- `@grid-columns`: This variable is used to define the maximum number of columns displayed on desktops and large screens. The default value is 12. However, by assigning a specific value, we can change the default value to less or more than 12, as per the requirement.

- `@grid-gutter-width`: This variable is the width of the gutter. The gutter is the vertical space between the grid columns, and the default value of the gutter width is 30 px.

- `@grid-float-breakpoint`: This variable is the minimum width with which the elements with the `col-lg-x` class start getting displayed in the columns. The default value of this attribute is the same as the minimum tablet screen width, which is 768 px.

Bootstrap Grid mixins

You can also create and modify the grid layout using the mixins in conjunction with variables defined in Bootstrap.

Let's take a look at the commonly used mixins in Bootstrap that are used to build semantic layouts:

- `.container-fixed()`: This mixin is used to create a container element centered on the page. The container will wrap rows and columns in our layouts.

- `.make-row()`: This mixin is used to create rows in our layouts. It clears all the CSS float declarations added to the columns wrapped in the row.

- `.make-column()`: This mixin is used to create columns in our layouts. It adds CSS float declarations to the columns, creates the gutters, and sets the column widths. It accepts one parameter that is the number of units for the column width with a default maximum of 12. The maximum can be changed by changing the value of the `@grid-columns` variable.

  An example is `.make-md-column(8);`

- `.make-column-offset()`: This mixin is used to add offsets to the columns. It accepts one parameter that is the number of units for the column offset with a default maximum of 12. The maximum can be changed by changing the value of the `@grid-columns` variable.

  An example is `.make-md-column-offset(1);`

- `.make-column-push()`: This mixin is used to move columns to the right. This is the same as using the `col-push-X` class. It accepts one parameter that is the number of units by which we can move the column with a default maximum of 12. The maximum can be changed by changing the value of the `@grid-columns` variable.

  An example is `.make-md-column-push(3);`

- `.make-column-pull()`: This mixin is used to move columns to the left. This is the same as using the `col-pull-X` class. It accepts one parameter that is the number of units by which we can move the column with a default maximum of 12. The maximum can be changed by changing the value of the `@grid-columns` variable.

  An example is `.make-md-column-pull(3);`

 Remember to add the prefix as per the screen size, that is, md for desktops, lg for large screens, sm for small screens, and xs for extra small screens in order to define the columns.

Creating a blog layout with the Bootstrap Grid mixins and variables

Let's create a blog layout using Bootstrap mixins and variables:

1. We start with a basic HTML document containing the Bootstrap CSS file. Then, we add the relevant content to it and move step by step in order to understand how it all works.

   Take a look at the following code to understand this better:

   ```html
   <!DOCTYPE html>
   <html>
     <head>
       <title>Using Bootstrap Grid Variables and Mixins
       </title>
   ```

```
<meta name="viewport" content="width=device-width,
initial-scale=1.0">
<link href="css/bootstrap.css" rel="stylesheet"
media="screen">
</head>
<body>
</body>
</html>
```

2. Now, let's define the blog document structure. In the `<header>` tag, we define the header with the blog title and description. Do not mix your thoughts about `<header>` with `<head>`; both are different. We define the `site-header` class for the header class:

```
<header class="site-header">
    <h1>Using variables and mixins to create a grid
    layout</h1>
</header>
```

3. Now that we have defined the blog title, we move on to the next part. At the bottom of the page, we add the copyright notice and assign the `site-footer` class to it:

```
<footer class="site-footer">
    Copyright &copy; 2014
</footer>
```

4. Both the footer and header will be wrapped in a root `<div>` element with the CSS class page. The blog post will be the `<article>` HTML5 element with the post title in a `<header>` element followed by the post content and all the post metadata in a `<footer>` element. We add the `"main"` ARIA role to the article to mark it as the main section of our HTML document.

 For readers who are unaware of ARIA and its roles, in-depth information can be found at `https://developer.mozilla.org/en-US/docs/Web/Accessibility/ARIA` and `http://www.w3.org/TR/wai-aria/roles`.

The full HTML code for the article will be the following:

```
<article role="main" >
  <header>
    <h2>Packt: Always finding a way</h2>
  </header>
  <div>
    <p>
```

```
            Packt is one of the most prolific and fast-growing
            tech book publishers in the world. Originally focused
            on open source software, Packt pays a royalty on
            relevant books directly to open source projects.
            These projects have received over $400,000 as part of
            Packt's Open Source Royalty Scheme to date.
        </p>
        <p>
            Our books focus on practicality, recognising that
            readers are ultimately concerned with getting the job
            done. Packt's digitally-focused business model allows
            us to publish up-to-date books in very specific
            areas.
        </p>
        <p>
            With over 1000 books published, Packt now offers a
            subscription service. This app and a PacktLib
            subscription now makes finding the information you
            need easier than ever before.
        </p>
    </div>
    <footer>
        <p>Posted on: 25-October-2014</p>
        <p>
            Tagged: Packt, PacktLib, Packt Mobile Browser App.
        </p>
    </footer>
</article>
```

5. The sidebar will show you the title of the recent posts and the date archives. They will be wrapped in a `<div>` element with the ARIA role complementary in order to show you that the sidebar is independent of but complementary to the main content. Each section of the sidebar will be put in an `<aside>` element and will use an `<h3>` element for its heading:

```
<div role="complementary">
    <aside>
    <h3>Recent Posts</h3>
    <ul>
        <li><a href="http://www.packtpub.com/news-center">
        Packt News Center </a></li>
        <li><a href="http://www.packtpub.com/support-
        complaints-and-feedback">Video Support</a></li>
        <li><a href="https://careers.packtpub.com/"> Packt
        Careers </a></li>
    </ul>
    </aside>
```

```
    <aside>
    <h3>Archives</h3>
    <ul>
        <li><a href="">March 2014</a></li>
        <li><a href="">June 2014</a></li>
        <li><a href="">July 2014</a></li>
    </ul>
    </aside>
</div>
```

6. The post and sidebar will be wrapped in a `<div>` element with the CSS class content, which we will put between the header and footer elements. The resulting HTML document will be the following:

```
<!DOCTYPE html>
<html>
<head>
  <title>Bootstrap Grid Variables and Mixins </title>
  <meta name="viewport" content="width=device-width,
  initial-scale=1.0">
  <link href="css/bootstrap.css" rel="stylesheet">
</head>
<body>
  <div class="page">
    <header class="site-header">
      <h1>Using variables and mixins to create a grid
      layout</h1>
    </header>
    <div class="content">
      <article role="main" >
        <header>
          <h2>Packt: Always finding a way</h2>
        </header>
        <div>
        <p>
          Packt is one of the most prolific and fast-
          growing tech book publishers in the world.
          Originally focused on open source software, Packt
          pays a royalty on relevant books directly to open
          source projects. These projects have received
          over $400,000 as part of Packt's Open Source
          Royalty Scheme to date.
        </p>
        <p>
```

```
    Our books focus on practicality, recognising that
    readers are ultimately concerned with getting the
    job done. Packt's digitally-focused business
    model allows us to publish up-to-date books in
    very specific areas.
  </p>
  <p>
    With over 1000 books published, Packt now offers
    a subscription service. This app and a PacktLib
    subscription now makes finding the information
    you need easier than ever before.
  </p>
</div>
<footer>
  <p>Posted on: 25-October-2014</p>
  <p>
    Tagged: Packt, PacktLib, Packt Mobile Browser
    App.
  </p>
</footer>

</article>
  <div role="complementary">
    <aside>
      <h3>Recent Posts</h3>
      <ul>
        <li><a href="http://www.packtpub.com/news-
        center"> Packt News Center </a></li>
        <li><a href="http://www.packtpub.com/support-
        complaints-and-feedback">Video
        Support</a></li>
        <li><a href="https://careers.packtpub.com/">
        Packt Careers </a></li>
      </ul>
    </aside>
    <aside>
      <h3>Archives</h3>
      <ul>
        <li><a href="">March 2014</a></li>
        <li><a href="">June 2014</a></li>
        <li><a href="">July 2014</a></li>
      </ul>
    </aside>
  </div>
```

```
      </div>

    <footer class="site-footer">
      Copyright &copy; 2014
    </footer>
  </div>
</body>
</html>
```

The output of the code upon execution will be as follows:

Using variables and mixins to create a grid layout

Packt: Always finding a way

Packt is one of the most prolific and fast-growing tech book publishers in the world. Originally focused on open source software, Packt pays a royalty on relevant books directly to open source projects. These projects have received over $400,000 as part of Packt's Open Source Royalty Scheme to date.

Our books focus on practicality, recognising that readers are ultimately concerned with getting the job done. Packt's digitally-focused business model allows us to publish up-to-date books in very specific areas.

With over 1000 books published, Packt now offers a subscription service. This app and a PacktLib subscription now makes finding the information you need easier than ever before.

Posted on: 25-October-2014

Tagged: Packt, PacktLib, Packt Mobile Browser App.

Recent Posts
- Packt News Center
- Video Support
- Packt Careers

Archives
- March 2014
- June 2014
- July 2014

Copyright © 2014

Styling the blog

We will now build the layout of the grid using some Bootstrap variables and mixins:

1. Create a `style.less` file in the `css` directory. Copy Bootstrap's `less` files from the unzipped source code folder and paste them into the `css` folder within a directory called `bootstrap`. The `css` folder will look as shown in the following screenshot:

Name	Date modified	Type	Size
bootstrap	29-10-2014 10:51	File folder	
bootstrap	05-08-2014 13:51	Cascading Style S...	130 KB
bootstrap.css.map	05-08-2014 13:51	MAP File	216 KB
bootstrap.min	05-08-2014 13:51	Cascading Style S...	107 KB
bootstrap-theme	05-08-2014 13:51	Cascading Style S...	21 KB
bootstrap-theme.css.map	05-08-2014 13:51	MAP File	23 KB
bootstrap-theme.min	05-08-2014 13:51	Cascading Style S...	19 KB
style	05-08-2014 14:16	LESS File	1 KB

2. The `bootstrap` file inside the `css` folder contains the `less` source code files, including the `bootstrap.less` file. The contents of the `bootstrap` folder inside the `css` folder will look as shown in the following screenshot:

Name	Date modified	Type	Size
mixins	14-08-2014 13:49	File folder	
.csscomb.json	14-08-2014 13:49	JSON File	8 KB
.csslintrc	14-08-2014 13:49	CSSLINTRC File	1 KB
alerts	14-08-2014 13:49	LESS File	2 KB
badges	14-08-2014 13:49	LESS File	2 KB
bootstrap	14-08-2014 13:49	LESS File	2 KB
breadcrumbs	14-08-2014 13:49	LESS File	1 KB
button-groups	14-08-2014 13:49	LESS File	6 KB
buttons	14-08-2014 13:49	LESS File	4 KB
carousel	14-08-2014 13:49	LESS File	5 KB
close	14-08-2014 13:49	LESS File	1 KB
code	14-08-2014 13:49	LESS File	2 KB
component-animations	14-08-2014 13:49	LESS File	1 KB
dropdowns	14-08-2014 13:49	LESS File	5 KB
forms	14-08-2014 13:49	LESS File	14 KB
glyphicons	14-08-2014 13:49	LESS File	15 KB
grid	14-08-2014 13:49	LESS File	2 KB
input-groups	14-08-2014 13:49	LESS Type	5 KB
jumbotron	14-08-2014 13:49	LESS File	1 KB
labels	14-08-2014 13:49	LESS File	2 KB
list-group	14-08-2014 13:49	LESS File	4 KB
media	14-08-2014 13:49	LESS File	1 KB

3. Open the `style.less` file in a notepad or your favorite editor. The next step will be to import `bootstrap.less` using the following line to include `bootstrap.less` file in it:

```
@import "bootstrap/bootstrap.less";
```

4. Then, we center the root `<div>` element (the element with the `.page` CSS class) on the screen and add some width to it. To center the element, we use the `.container-fixed()` Bootstrap mixin. This is the one that Bootstrap uses internally in the `.container` CSS class. We add the mixin in our LESS file as follows:

```
.page {
   .container-fixed();
}
```

After we add the mixin to the root `<div>` element, the element will still occupy the full width of the screen. This behavior is desirable on phone screens, but it's not what we want on tablets and desktop screens.

5. We then set the maximum width to 728 px for tablets and 940 px for desktop screens by targeting these device screens with Media Queries.

The following LESS code will target the tablets. Notice the use of the `@screen-tablet` LESS variable, which is used by Bootstrap to avoid hardcoding the tablet width everywhere. By using the `@screen-tablet` variable, the value can be easily changed in the future without having to find every instance where it's used:

```
@media screen and (min-width: @screen-tablet) {
   .page {
     max-width: 728px;
   }
}
```

6. To set the maximum width on the desktop, we add the following code to our `style.less` file. We use the `@screen-desktop` variable for the desktop width in the same vein as `@screen-tablet` is used in the preceding code:

```
@media screen and (min-width: @screen-desktop) {
   .page {
     max-width: 940px;
   }
```

There are other variables that are used by Bootstrap to specify the screen widths:

- For phone screens, there's the `@screen-phone` variable, which is an alias of `@screen-tiny`. Its default value is 480 px.

- For tablet screens, there's the `@screen-tablet` variable, which is an alias of `@screen-small`. Its default value is 768 px.

- For desktop screens, there's the `@screen-desktop` variable, which is an alias of `@screen-medium`. Its default value is 992 px.

- For large desktop screens, there's the `@screen-large-desktop` variable, which is an alias of `@screen-large`. Its default value is 1200 px.

7. After centering and adding a width to the root element, we align the blog post and sidebar in two columns. The blog post will be in the left column, while the sidebar will be in the right one.

   We make the `<div>` element that is wrapping the blog post and sidebar behave like the default Bootstrap row using the Bootstrap mixin.

   The `.make-column()` Bootstrap mixin will be used to create the columns. It accepts one parameter, which is the number of grid units that the column will take.

   For example, `.make-md-column(6)` will make the element where the mixin is added span 6 units for desktops. This is the same as adding the `col-md-6` CSS class.

   We will also use the `.make-column-offset()` Bootstrap mixin to add offsets to columns. It also accepts a parameter. The `.make-md-column-offset(1)` attribute is the same as using the `col-md-offset-1` CSS class.

8. We set the width of the blog post column to 8 units and the width of the sidebar to 3 units. We also add an offset of 1 unit to the sidebar:

```
article[role=main] {
  .make-md-column(8);
}

div[role=complementary] {
  .make-md-column(3);
  .make-md-column-offset(1);
}
```

Now, the columns have been created.

9. Next, we need to align the header and footer. Therefore, we will add paddings to their left and right. The paddings will be half the width of gutter:

```
.site-header,
.site-footer {
  padding-left:  (@grid-gutter-width / 2);
  padding-right: (@grid-gutter-width / 2);
}
```

10. We also add a padding to the top of the footer in order to separate it from the content area:

```
.site-footer {
  padding-top: 30px;
}
```

Now that we have used all the styles we needed, let's take a look at the style.less file:

```
@import "bootstrap/bootstrap.less";

.page {
  .container-fixed();
}

@media screen and (min-width: @screen-tablet) {
  .page {
    max-width: 728px;
  }
}

@media screen and (min-width: @screen-desktop) {
  .page {
    max-width: 940px;
  }
}

.content {
  .make-row();
}

article[role=main] {
  .make-md-column(8);
}
```

```less
div[role=complementary] {
    .make-md-column(3);
    .make-md-column-offset(1);
}

.site-header,
.site-footer {
    padding-left:  (@grid-gutter-width / 2);
    padding-right: (@grid-gutter-width / 2);
}

.site-footer {
    padding-top: 30px;
}
```

11. Using WinLess, we will convert the `style.less` file to `style.css` in a manner that is similar to how we converted the LESS file to CSS in *Chapter 2*, *Installing and Customizing Bootstrap*. Then, we will include the `style.css` file in our main HTML document after including the `bootstrap.css` file, as we need `style.css` to override the default bootstrap code.

    Thus, the initial part of the HTML document will look like this:

```
Grid_Mixins_Variables_Creating Blog Layout - Notepad

File  Edit  Format  View  Help

<!DOCTYPE html>
<html>
<head>
    <title>Bootstrap Grid Variables and Mixins </title>
    <meta name="viewport" content="width=device-width, initial-scale=1.0">
    <link href="css/bootstrap.css" rel="stylesheet">
    <link href="css/style.css" rel="stylesheet">
</head>
<body>
    <div class="page">
      <header class="site-header">
              <h1>Using variables and mixins to create a grid layout</h1>
      </header>
        <div class="content">
          <article role="main" >
            <header>
              <h2>Packt: Always finding a way</h2>
            </header>
            <div>
```

The output of the code upon execution will be as follows:

Using variables and mixins to create a grid layout

Packt: Always finding a way

Packt is one of the most prolific and fast-growing tech book publishers in the world. Originally focused on open source software, Packt pays a royalty on relevant books directly to open source projects. These projects have received over $400,000 as part of Packt's Open Source Royalty Scheme to date.

Our books focus on practicality, recognising that readers are ultimately concerned with getting the job done. Packt's digitally-focused business model allows us to publish up-to-date books in very specific areas.

With over 1000 books published, Packt now offers a subscription service. This app and a PacktLib subscription now makes finding the information you need easier than ever before.

Posted on: 25-October-2014

Tagged: Packt, PacktLib, Packt Mobile Browser App.

Copyright © 2014

Recent Posts

- Packt News Center
- Video Support
- Packt Careers

Archives

- March 2014
- June 2014
- July 2014

You have now learned how to use variables and mixins to create a semantic layout.

Summary

In this chapter, we had a look at the Grid classes. We understood the process of adding rows and columns in addition to adding offsets to columns. We also had a look at reversing the order of columns and how columns are nested within each other. We also learned about the commonly used variables and mixins that are used to create a semantic layout. Finally, we created a custom blog layout with the Bootstrap variables and mixins with our own semantic elements and classes using a comprehensive, practical example.

In the next chapter, we will show you how to use the Bootstrap Base CSS elements by adapting a practical approach, including numerous code examples, to help you get to grips with the various styles in order to streamline your web designing experience.

4
Using the Base CSS

Applying consistent styling to HTML elements such as headings, paragraphs, tables, and forms is generally easy but a time-consuming process. In addition to including `Normalize.css` (http://necolas.github.io/normalize.css/) to render HTML elements consistently across browsers and in line with modern web standards, Bootstrap provides default styling for typography, code, tables, forms, buttons, and image elements.

In this chapter, we will see how to use the Bootstrap Base CSS in your HTML pages and how to customize it.

We will cover the following in this chapter:

- Implementing the Bootstrap Base CSS
- Customizing the Bootstrap Base CSS using LESS variables

If you want to use the Bootstrap Base CSS as it is, with no customization, you can simply include the Bootstrap CSS in your HTML files using the link tag:

```
<link href="css/bootstrap.min.css" rel="stylesheet"
media="screen">
```

Implementing the Bootstrap Base CSS

In this section, we will take a look at the default styles used in the Bootstrap Base CSS listed as follows:

- Headings
- Body copy
- Inline elements
- Alignment classes

- Addresses
- Blockquotes
- Lists
- Tables
- Buttons
- Forms
- Code
- Images
- Font styles

Instead of wandering through loads of theory, you will learn the Base CSS practically by using numerous code examples.

Headings

Bootstrap headings include sizes that are multiples of the default ones:

- Heading level 1 `<h1>`: It has a default font size of 38 px, which is approximately 2.70 times the default base font size of 14 px

- Heading level 2 `<h2>`: It has a default font size of 32 px, which is approximately 2.25 times the default base font size of 14 px

- Heading level 3 `<h3>`: It has a default font size of 24 px, which is approximately 1.70 times the default base font size of 14 px

- Heading level 4 `<h4>`: It has a default font size of 18 px, which is approximately 1.25 times the default base font size of 14 px

- Heading level 5 `<h5>`: It has the same font size (14 px) as the default base font size

- Heading level 6 `<h6>`: It has a default font size of 12 px, which is approximately 0.85 times the default base font size of 14 px

In almost all the code examples, we have used the padding style between the `<style>` tags in the `<head>` section to improve the aesthetics. The padding style helps you to observe the output better, as it is not close to the left side of the screen.

Take a look at the following code to understand it better:

```html
<!DOCTYPE html>
<html>
<head>
  <title> Headings in Bootstrap CSS </title>
  <meta name="viewport" content="width=device-width, initial-
    scale=1.0">
  <link href="css/bootstrap.css" rel="stylesheet" media="screen">
  <style>
    #packtpub
      {
        padding-top: 25px;
        padding-bottom: 25px;
        padding-right: 50px;
        padding-left: 50px;
      }
  </style>
</head>
<body id="packtpub">
  <h1> Packt: Always finding a way </h1>
  <h2> Packt: Always finding a way </h2>
  <h3> Packt: Always finding a way </h3>
  <h4> Packt: Always finding a way </h4>
  <h5> Packt: Always finding a way </h5>
  <h6> Packt: Always finding a way </h6>
</body>
</html>
```

The output of this code upon execution will be as follows:

After observing the code and the preceding screenshot, you can explicitly see the implementation of the headings and the size of the font. In addition to this, the classes from h1 to h6 can be used to match the font styling of a heading and help you to display your text inline.

Take a look at the following code snippet to see how it works:

```
<body id="packtpub">
    <div class="h1">h1. Packt: Always finding a way </div>
    <div class="h2">h2. Packt: Always finding a way </div>
    <div class="h3">h3. Packt: Always finding a way </div>
    <div class="h4">h4. Packt: Always finding a way </div>
    <div class="h5">h5. Packt: Always finding a way </div>
    <div class="h6">h6. Packt: Always finding a way </div>
</body>
```

The output of the code upon execution will be as follows:

h1. Packt: Always finding a way

h2. Packt: Always finding a way

h3. Packt: Always finding a way

h4. Packt: Always finding a way

h5. Packt: Always finding a way

h6. Packt: Always finding a way

You can also add texts with smaller font sizes within headings using the <small> tag. The font sizes of the <small> tag in headings are as follows:

- Small text in <h1>: The default font size is 24 px, which is approximately 1.70 times the default base font size of 14 px

- Small text in <h2>: The default font size is 18 px, which is approximately 1.25 times the default base font size of 14 px

- Small text in <h3>: The default font size is 14 px, which is the same as the base font size

- Small text in <h4>: The default font size is also 14 px

Take a look at the following code example to understand it better:

```html
<!DOCTYPE html>
<html>
<head>
  <title> Headings in Bootstrap CSS </title>
  <meta name="viewport" content="width=device-width, initial-
  scale=1.0">
  <link href="css/bootstrap.css" rel="stylesheet" media="screen">
  <style>
    #packtpub {
      padding-top: 25px;
      padding-bottom: 25px;
      padding-right: 50px;
      padding-left: 50px;
    }
  </style>
</head>
<body id="packtpub">
  <h1> Packt: <small> Always finding a way </small></h1>
  <h2> Packt: <small> Always finding a way </small></h2>
  <h3> Packt: <small> Always finding a way </small></h3>
  <h4> Packt: <small> Always finding a way </small></h4>
  <h5> Packt: <small> Always finding a way </small></h5>
  <h6> Packt: <small> Always finding a way </small></h6>
</body>
</html>
```

The output of the code upon execution will be as follows:

As you can see, the text defined within the `<small>` tag is lighter and smaller than the actual heading style.

Body copy

Bootstrap defines a lead paragraph as a paragraph that stands out from others. It does so by increasing its bottom margin and font size and decreasing its font weight and line height.

The bottom margin of a lead paragraph is 2 times the bottom margin of a normal paragraph. Its font size is 1.5 times the font size of a normal paragraph, thus 1.5 times the base font size.

The value of the font weight of a lead paragraph is 200 and the value of the line height is 1.4.

To create a lead paragraph, add the `lead` class to any paragraph.

Take a look at the following code so that you understand it better:

```
<!DOCTYPE html>
<html>
<head>
  <title> The lead class </title>
  <meta name="viewport" content="width=device-width, initial-
  scale=1.0">
  <link href="css/bootstrap.css" rel="stylesheet" media="screen">
</head>
  <p> Packt has a dedicated customer service department to respond
  to your questions. </p>
  <br>
  <p class="lead">
  Packt's mission is to help the world put software to work in new
  ways
  </p>
</html>
```

The output of this code upon execution will be as follows:

Packt has a dedicated customer service department to respond to your questions.

Packt's mission is to help the world put software to work in new ways

Typographic elements

Bootstrap provides consistent styling across browsers for common typographic elements. You can use them to semantically enhance your website copy. These HTML elements are emphasis inline elements, alignment and emphasis classes, abbreviations, addresses, blockquotes, and lists.

Emphasis inline elements

Bootstrap has default styling for the following emphasis elements:

- `<strong>`: The font weight of any text between the HTML `<strong>` tags is set to bold. This element can be used to give some text more importance in the surrounding paragraph. The `<strong>` element should not be confounded with the `<b>` element, which doesn't have any semantic meaning.

- `<em>`: The HTML `<em>` element is used to add stress emphasis to a body of text. Bootstrap sets its font style to italic. The `<em>` element should not be confounded with the HTML `<i>` element, which doesn't have any semantic meaning.

- `<mark>`: The `<mark>` element is used to highlight text that is used for reference purposes due to its relevance in another context.

- `<u>`: The `<u>` tag is used to underline text. It can be used to emphasize important terms or for labeling the text which is of significance.

- `<del>`: The `<del>` tag is used to indicate blocks of text that have been deleted from a document. It is rendered through strike-through text.

Take a look at the following code to understand it better:

```
<!DOCTYPE html>
<html>
<head>
  <title>Emphasis elements</title>
  <meta name="viewport" content="width=device-width, initial-scale=1.0">
  <link href="css/bootstrap.css" rel="stylesheet" media="screen">
  <style>
    #packt {
      padding-top: 25px;
      padding-bottom: 25px;
      padding-right: 50px;
      padding-left: 50px;
    }
```

```
    </style>
  </head>
  <body id="packt">
    <p>
      <u> Packt Publishing </u><br>
      Founded in 2004 in <strong> Birmingham, UK </strong>, Packt's
      mission is to help the world put software to work in new ways.
    </p>
    <p> Packt achieves it due to the <mark> delivery of effective
      learning and information services </mark>to IT professionals.
    </p>
    <p> Working towards that vision, <del>we have published over
    2000 books and videos </del> so far. </p>
    <p>We have also awarded over $1,000,000 through our <em> Open
    Source Project Royalty scheme. </em></p>
  </body>
</html>
```

The output of the code upon execution will be as follows:

As you can see from the output, the emphasis elements help you to implement inline styles to make relevant text stand out significantly.

Alignment classes

Bootstrap has three CSS classes to align text to the left, right, or center of its parent block element. These CSS classes are:

- `text-left`: As the name indicates, this CSS class aligns the text to the left of its parent block element. It's the same as applying the `text-align` CSS property with the value `left` to the element.

- `text-right`: This aligns the text to the right of the parent block element. It provides the same result as applying the `text-align` CSS property with the value `right` to the element.

- `text-center`: This aligns the text horizontally at the center of its parent block element. This provides the same result as applying the `text-align` CSS property with the value `center` to the element.

  In addition to these three classes, we also have the `text-justify` class.

- `text-justify`: This stretches the lines so that each line has equal width similar to the justification of text in newspapers or a Word document.

Take a look at the following code to understand it better:

```html
<!DOCTYPE html>
<html>
<head>
  <title>Alignment Classes</title>
  <meta name="viewport" content="width=device-width, initial-scale=1.0">
  <link href="css/bootstrap.css" rel="stylesheet" media="screen">
  <style>
    #packt {
      padding-top: 25px;
      padding-bottom: 25px;
      padding-right: 50px;
      padding-left: 50px;
    }
  </style>
</head>

<div id="packt">
  <p class="text-left">Packt Publishing</p>
  <p class="text-center">Packt: Always finding a way</p>
  <p class="text-right"> Packt Online library</p>
  <p class="text-justify"> Founded in 2004 in Birmingham, UK,
  Packt's mission is to help the world put software to work in new
  ways, through the delivery of effective learning and information
  services to IT professionals.</p>
</div>
</html>
```

The output of this code upon execution will be:

Packt Publishing

Packt: Always finding a way

Packt Online library

Founded in 2004 in Birmingham, UK, Packt's mission is to help the world put software to work in new ways, through the delivery of effective learning and information services to IT professionals.

As you can see from the output, the alignment of the text was as it was defined in the preceding code.

Emphasis classes

Bootstrap provides CSS classes that change the color of text to indicate a special meaning. These classes are:

- `text-muted`: This changes the color of the text to a light gray shade set by the `@gray-light` LESS variable. It can be used to diminish the importance of a text.

- `text-warning`: This changes the color of the text to the orange shade set by the `@state-warning-text` LESS variable. It can be used to indicate warning or something that is going to have incorrect consequences.

- `text-danger`: This changes the color of the text to the red shade set by the `@state-danger-text` LESS variable. It can be used to indicate a dangerous action, a problem, or an error that can be crucial.

- `text-success`: This changes the color of the text to the green shade set by the `@state-success-text` LESS variable. It can be used to indicate success after an action such as a form submission.

- `text-info`: This changes the color of the text to the blue shade set by the `@state-info-text` LESS variable. It can be used to indicate general information that can be quite handy.

- `text-primary`: This changes the color of the text to a sky blue shade. It is usually used to indicate text that is relevant based on priority.

Take a look at the following code so that you understand it better:

```html
<!DOCTYPE html>
<html>
<head>
  <title>Emphasis Classes</title>
  <meta name="viewport" content="width=device-width, initial-
  scale=1.0">
  <link href="css/bootstrap.css" rel="stylesheet" media="screen">
  <style>
    #packt {
      padding-top: 25px;
      padding-bottom: 25px;
      padding-right: 50px;
      padding-left: 50px;
    }
  </style>

</head>
<body id ="packt">
  <p class="text-muted"> Bootstrap 2 is outdated </p>
  <p class="text-primary"> Bootstrap 3 is the present version</p>
  <p class="text-success"> Bootstrap is an awesome toolkit for web
  design </p>
  <p class="text-info"> Bootstrap 4 is expected to be among the
  forthcoming releases </p>
  <p class="text-warning">Don't mess with me </p>
  <p class="text-danger"> Step with caution </p>
</body>
</html>
```

The output of this code upon execution will be as follows:

Bootstrap 2 is outdated

Bootstrap 3 is the present version

Bootstrap is an awesome toolkit for web design

Bootstrap 4 is expected to be among the forthcoming releases

Don't mess with me

Step with caution

Similar to contextual colors for text, you can also use colors to set the background of an element using the following classes:

- `bg-primary`
- `bg-success`
- `bg-info`
- `bg-warning`
- `bg-danger`

Suppose we remove the contextual colors for text and replace it with contextual background colors, we will see the following output (refer to the code bundle for the entire code):

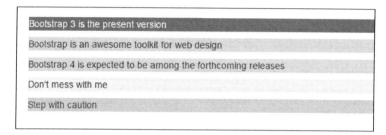

Addresses

Addresses should be depicted using the HTML element `address`. According to the HTML specification, the `address` element should be used for contact information related to the nearest article or body element. Arbitrary addresses not related to contact information should be displayed using the HTML element `p` instead of the element `address`.

Take a look at the following code to understand it better:

```
<!DOCTYPE html>
<html>
<head>
  <title>Address</title>
  <meta name="viewport" content="width=device-width, initial-
  scale=1.0">
  <link href="css/bootstrap.css" rel="stylesheet" media="screen">

  <style>
    #packt {
      padding-top: 25px;
      padding-bottom: 25px;
```

```
      padding-right: 50px;
      padding-left: 50px;
    }
  </style>

</head>
<body>
  <address id="packt">
    <strong> Packt Publishing Limited. </strong><br>
    Livery Place, 35 Livery Street,<br>
    Birmingham, West Midlands, B3 2PB<br>
    <a href="mailto:contact@packtpub.com"> Contact us </a>
  </address>
</body>
</html>
```

The output of this code will be as follows:

Packt Publishing Limited.
Livery Place, 35 Livery Street,
Birmingham, West Midlands, B3 2PB
Contact us

As you can see from the output, the address for **Packt Publishing Limited** is defined within the `<address>` HTML tag in Bootstrap.

Blockquotes

Blockquotes are used to indicate the enclosed text that originates from another source. They are displayed by placing an HTML paragraph element p between a `blockquote` element.

Bootstrap adds a large border of 5 pixels to the left of blockquotes as shown in the screenshot following the code. The color of the border is a light gray set by the `@gray-lighter` LESS variable.

Take a look at the following code to understand it better:

```
<!DOCTYPE html>
<html>
<head>
  <title>Blockquotes</title>
```

```
      <meta name="viewport" content="width=device-width, initial-
      scale=1.0">
      <link href="css/bootstrap.css" rel="stylesheet" media="screen">
  </head>
    <blockquote>
      <p>
      If you are a CakePHP developer looking to ease the burden of
      development, then this book is for you.
      </p>
      <small>CakePHP 2 Application Cookbook <cite title="Source
      Title">by James Watts, Jorge González</cite></small>
    </blockquote>
  </html>
```

The output of this code upon execution will be as follows:

> If you are a CakePHP developer looking to ease the burden of development, then this book is for you.
>
> — CakePHP 2 Application Cookbook by James Watts, Jorge González

If you look at the output and the preceding code, you will observe that the source of the quote is defined between the `<small>` tags and the name of the source is defined within the `<cite>` tags.

If you need right-aligned content, then you can also use the `blockquote-reverse` class.

Take a look at the following code example to understand this better:

```
<!DOCTYPE html>
<html>
<head>
  <title>Blockquote Reverse</title>
  <meta name="viewport" content="width=device-width, initial-
  scale=1.0">
  <link href="css/bootstrap.css" rel="stylesheet" media="screen">

</head>
<blockquote class="blockquote-reverse">
  <p>If you are a CakePHP developer looking to ease the burden of
  development, then this book is for you.</p>
  <small>CakePHP 2 Application Cookbook <cite title="Source
  Title">by James Watts, Jorge González</cite></small>
</blockquote>
</html>
```

The output of the code on execution will be as follows:

> If you are a CakePHP developer looking to ease the burden of development, then this book is for you.
>
> CakePHP 2 Application Cookbook by James Watts, Jorge González —

From the preceding output, you can clearly see that the blockquote text content is aligned to the right.

Abbreviations

Abbreviations should be displayed using the HTML element `abbr`. Bootstrap adds a light gray, dotted border at the bottom of abbreviations with a title attribute. It also adds a help cursor that appears on hovering over abbreviations.

Bootstrap also provides the `initialism` CSS class, which decreases the font size of the abbreviation to 90 percent of the parent font size and transforms its letters to uppercase.

If an abbreviation doesn't have a `title` attribute or a `initialism` class added, Bootstrap won't apply any style to it.

The following code contains two abbreviations. The second one has the `initialism` CSS class added:

```
<!DOCTYPE html>
<html>
<head>
  <title> Bootstrap Abbreviations </title>
  <meta name="viewport" content="width=device-width, initial-
  scale=1.0">
  <link href="css/bootstrap.css" rel="stylesheet" media="screen">
  <style>
    #packt {
      padding-top: 25px;
      padding-bottom: 25px;
      padding-right: 50px;
      padding-left: 50px;
    }
  </style>
</head>
<body id="packt">
  <p>An abbreviation of the word attribute is
  <abbr title="attribute">attr</abbr>.</p>
```

```
   <p>An abbreviation of the expression Hypertext Markup Language
   is <abbr title="Hypertext Markup Language"
   class="initialism">html</abbr>.</p>
  </body>
 </html>
```

The output of this code will be as follows:

An abbreviation of the word attribute is attr.

An abbreviation of the expression Hypertext Markup Language is HTML.

If you hover over **HTML**, you can see the following screen:

An abbreviation of the word attribute is attr.

An abbreviation of the expression Hypertext Markup Language is HTML.

Hypertext Markup Language

As you can see from the output, on hovering, you can see the complete expression that HTML stands for as defined in the code.

Lists

Bootstrap harmonizes the margins and paddings of unordered, ordered, and description lists. It also provides CSS classes that can be used to remove the default styling of lists or display list items inline.

Take a look at the following code to help you understand it better:

```
<!DOCTYPE html>
<html>
<head>
  <title>Ordered and Unordered Lists </title>
  <meta name="viewport" content="width=device-width, initial-
  scale=1.0">
  <link href="css/bootstrap.css" rel="stylesheet" media="screen">
  <style>
    #packt {
```

```
        padding-top: 25px;
        padding-bottom: 25px;
        padding-right: 50px;
        padding-left: 50px;
      }
    </style>
  </head>
  <body id="packt">
    <h1> Packt Publishing </h1>
    <ul>
      <li> Packt Categories </li>
      <li> Packt Subscription Services </li>
      <ul>
        <li> Mobile Browser App </li>
        <li> PacktLib: Online Library </li>
      </ul>
      <li> News Center</li>
      <li>Packt Blog</li>
    </ul>
    <h1> Reader's space </h1>
    <ol>
      <li> Packt Tech Hub </li>
      <li> Article Network </li>
      <li> Support </li>
      <li> About us </li>
    </ol>
  </body>
</html>
```

The output of this code will be as follows:

Packt Publishing

- Packt Categories
- Packt Subscription Services
    - Mobile Browser App
    - PacktLib: Online Library
- News Center
- Packt Blog

Reader's space

1. Packt Tech Hub
2. Article Network
3. Support
4. About us

While unordered lists are those in which the order doesn't matter, ordered lists are those where the hierarchy is maintained as defined. While unordered lists are defined by the `<ul>` tags, ordered lists are defined by the `<ol>` tags. Also, from the preceding code and the output, you can see that we have nested unordered lists within the main unordered lists resulting in the **Mobile Browser App** and **PacktLib: Online Library** text nested under the main lists.

You can also use unstyled lists if you need to.

Take a look at the following code to understand this better:

```
<!DOCTYPE html>
<html>
<head>
  <title>Ordered and Unordered Lists </title>
  <meta name="viewport" content="width=device-width, initial-
  scale=1.0">
  <link href="css/bootstrap.css" rel="stylesheet" media="screen">
  <style>
    #packt {
      padding-top: 25px;
      padding-bottom: 25px;
      padding-right: 50px;
      padding-left: 50px;
    }
  </style>
</head>
<body id="packt">
  <h1> Packt Publishing </h1>
  <ul class="list-unstyled">
    <li> About us </li>
    <li> Packt Categories </li>
    <li> Packt Subscription Services </li>
    <ul>
      <li> Mobile Browser App </li>
      <li> PacktLib: Online Library </li>
    </ul>
    <li> News Center</li>
    <li>Packt Blog</li>
  </ul>

  <h1> Reader's space </h1>
  <ol>
    <li> Packt Categories </li>
    <ol class="list-unstyled">
```

```
        <li> Web development </li>
        <li> Application development </li>
        <li> Big Data </li>
        <li> Networking and Servers </li>
        <li> Virtualization and cloud </li>
      </ol>
      <li> Packt Tech Hub </li>
      <li> Article Network </li>
      <li> Support </li>
    </ol>
  </body>
</html>
```

The output of the code on execution will be as follows:

If you observe the output, you can see that in the unordered lists, the main list comprising **About us**, **Packt Categories**, **Packt Subscription Services**, **News Center**, and **Packt Blog** do not have any styles applied resulting in no bullet points. However, the nested text list **Mobile Browser App** and **PacktLib: Online Library** have bullet points meaning that you need to add the `list-unstyled` class to nested elements too explicitly. Under **Reader's space**, we can see that the nested ordered lists under **Packt Categories** have an unstyled list without any bullets as we have defined the `list-unstyled` class for the nested elements.

You can also list items on a single line by using the `list-inline` class.

Take a look at the following code snippet to understand it better:

```
<body>
  <ul class="list-inline" id="packt">
    <li> Web development </li>
    <li> Application Development </li>
    <li> Big Data and Business Intelligence </li>
    <li> Virtualization and Cloud </li>
    <li> Networking and Servers </li>
  </ul>
</body>
```

The output of the code on execution will be as follows:

Web development   Application Development   Big Data and Business Intelligence   Virtualization and Cloud   Networking and Servers

As you can see, the list items have been displayed inline as defined.

Tables

Bootstrap provides an efficient layout to build elegant tables, which you will learn about in the following section.

Basic styling

To use the basic table styling provided by Bootstrap, you need to add the `table` CSS class to the HTML `table` tags in your code.

Take a look at the following code example:

```
<!DOCTYPE html>
<html>
<head>
  <title>Bootstrap Tables</title>
  <meta name="viewport" content="width=device-width, initial-
  scale=1.0">

  <link href="css/bootstrap.css" rel="stylesheet" media="screen">
  <style>
```

```
      #packt {
        padding-top: 25px;
        padding-bottom: 25px;
        padding-right: 50px;
        padding-left: 50px;
      }
    </style>

</head>
<body id="packt">
  <table class="table ">
    <thead>
      <tr>
        <th>First Name</th>
        <th>Last Name</th>
        <th>Role</th>
      </tr>
    </thead>
    <tbody>
      <tr>
        <td>Aravind </td>
        <td>Shenoy</td>
        <td>Technical Content Writer</td>
      </tr>
      <tr>
        <td>Jim</td>
        <td>Morrison</td>
        <td>Awesome Vocalist</td>
      </tr>
      <tr>
        <td>Jimi</td>
        <td>Hendrix</td>
        <td> Amazing Guitarist</td>
      </tr>

    </tbody>
  </table>
</body>
</html>
```

The output of the code will be as follows:

First Name	Last Name	Role
Aravind	Shenoy	Technical Content Writer
Jim	Morrison	Awesome Vocalist
Jimi	Hendrix	Amazing Guitarist

You can set the background color of the tables by changing the value of the `@table-bg` LESS variable. Its default value is transparent. You can also use the CSS classes, `table-bordered` and `table-striped`, to implement borders and zebra striping to the tables.

Take a look at the following code snippet to understand it better:

```
<body id="packt">
    <table class="table table-bordered table-striped">
        <thead>
          <tr>
            <th>First Name</th>
            <th>Last Name</th>
            <th>Role</th>
          </tr>
        </thead>
        <tbody>
          <tr>
            <td>Aravind </td>
            <td>Shenoy</td>
            <td>Technical Content Writer</td>
          </tr>
          <tr>
            <td>Jim</td>
            <td>Morrison</td>
            <td>Awesome vocalist</td>
          </tr>
          <tr>
            <td>Jimi</td>
            <td>Hendrix</td>
            <td> Amazing Guitarist</td>
          </tr>

        </tbody>
    </table>
</body>
```

The output of this code upon execution will be as follows:

First Name	Last Name	Role
Aravind	Shenoy	Technical Content Writer
Jim	Morrison	Awesome vocalist
Jimi	Hendrix	Amazing Guitarist

From the preceding code and its output, you can see that the borders and stripes are applied to the table. The color of the stripes is set with the built-in LESS variable @table-bg-accent. Its default value is #f9f9f9. The color of the borders is set with the built-in LESS variable @table-border-color. To enable a hover state on table rows, add the class table-hover to your tables. The background color of the row on hover is set by the built-in LESS variable @table-bg-hover. To make your tables more compact, you can use the table-condensed class.

You can also add contextual colors to the tables or even individual cells by using classes such as success, warning, danger, info, and active; for example, let's define the contextual classes to the table rows as shown in the following code snippet:

```html
<body id="packt">
    <table class="table ">
      <thead >
        <tr>
          <th>First Name</th>
          <th>Last Name</th>
          <th>Role</th>
        </tr>
      </thead>
      <tbody>
        <tr class="success">
          <td>Aravind </td>
          <td>Shenoy</td>
          <td>Technical Content Writer</td>
        </tr>
        <tr class ="info">
          <td>Jim</td>
          <td>Morrison</td>
          <td>Awesome Vocalist</td>
```

```
      </tr>
      <tr class="active">
        <td>Jimi</td>
        <td>Hendrix</td>
        <td> Amazing Guitarist</td>
      </tr>

    </tbody>
  </table>
</body>
```

The output of the code will be as follows:

First Name	Last Name	Role
Aravind	Shenoy	Technical Content Writer
Jim	Morrison	Awesome Vocalist
Jimi	Hendrix	Amazing Guitarist

Buttons

You can create buttons and define contextual colors for each of them. You can also define the size of the button. In Bootstrap, you can also define an active or disabled state for the button. You can use button classes on the `<a>` or `<input>` element though it is preferable to use the `< button>` element for appropriate semantics.

Take a look at the following code to understand it better:

```
<!DOCTYPE html>
<html>
<head>
  <title>Buttons in Bootstrap</title>
  <meta name="viewport" content="width=device-width, initial-
  scale=1.0">
  <link href="css/bootstrap.css" rel="stylesheet" media="screen">
  <style>
    #packt {
      padding-top: 25px;
      padding-bottom: 25px;
      padding-right: 50px;
      padding-left: 50px;
    }
  </style>
</head>
```

```
<body id="packt">
  <h1> <u> Different kinds of buttons in Bootstrap </u1> </h1>
  <br>
    <button type="button" class="btn btn-default">Default
    Button</button>
  <br><br>
    <button type="button" class="btn btn-primary">Primary
    Button</button>
  <br><br>
    <button type="button" class="btn btn-success btn-lg">Success
Button</button>
  <br><br>
    <button type="button" class="btn btn-info btn-sm">Info
    Button</button>
  <br><br>
    <button type="button" class="btn btn-warning btn-xs">Warning
    Button</button>
  <br><br>
    <button type="button" class="btn btn-danger">Danger
    Button</button>
  <br><br>
    <button type="button" class="btn btn-link">Link
    Button</button>
</body>
</html>
```

The output of this code will be as follows:

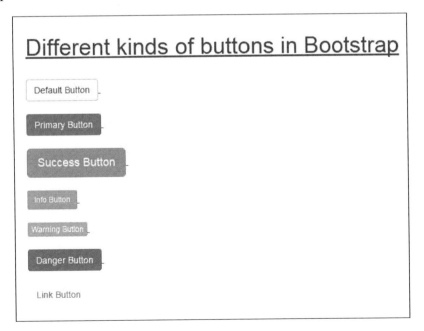

As you can see, the contextual colors are applied to the buttons. You can also see that **Success Button**, **Info Button**, and **Warning Button** are of different sizes than the others as we have defined `btn-lg`, `btn-sm`, and `btn-xs` for them.

Forms

Forms fields are automatically styled by Bootstrap. Forms can be defined as normal, inline, and horizontal as per the requirement.

Take a look at the following code to understand it better:

```
<!DOCTYPE html>
<html>
<head>
  <title>Forms in Bootstrap</title>
  <meta name="viewport" content="width=device-width, initial-
  scale=1.0">
  <link href="css/bootstrap.css" rel="stylesheet" media="screen">
  <style>
    #packt {
      padding-top: 25px;
      padding-bottom: 25px;
      padding-right: 50px;
      padding-left: 50px;
    }
  </style>
</head>
<body id="packt">
  <form role="form">
    <div class="form-group">
      <label for="enterusername"> Enter Email Address as the
      Username</label>
      <input type="email" class="form-control" id="enterusername"
      placeholder="Enter email">
    </div>
    <div class="form-group">
      <label for="enterpassword">Password</label>
      <input type="password" class="form-control"
      id="enterpassword" placeholder="Password">
    </div>
    <br>
    <div class="form-group">
      <label for="filebrowse">Browse to find file</label>
      <input type="file" id="filebrowse">
    </div>
    <br>
    <div class="checkbox">
      <label> <input type="checkbox"> Keep me signed in </label>
    </div>
```

```
      <br>
      <div class="radio">
        <label>
          <input type="radio" name="optionsRadios" value="option1"
          id="radio1">
          Male
        </label>
      </div>

      <div class="radio">
        <label>
          <input type="radio" name="optionsRadios" value="option2"
          id="radio2">
          Female
        </label>
      </div>
      <br>
      <button type="submit" class="btn btn-default">Login</button>
  </form>
</body>
</html>
```

The output of this code upon execution will be as follows:

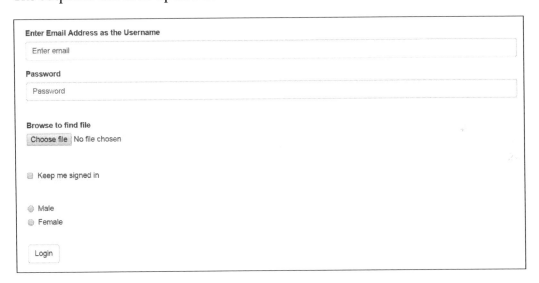

As we can see in the output, you can create a form in Bootstrap. In the preceding code, we have defined the form groups and then combined the essential elements together, including defining the labels in addition to creating the radio and checkbox types.

Inline forms

Forms can also be displayed inline with the input displayed next to each other. To display the inputs inline, you need to add the `form-inline` class to the form and set a width value to the input box because the default width is 100 percent.

Take a look at the following code block defined in the HTML document to understand it better:

```html
<body id="packt">
  <form role="form" class="form-inline">
    <div class="form-group">
      <label for="emailaddress" class="sr-only">Email
      Address</label>
      <input type="email" class="form-control" id="emailaddress"
      placeholder="Enter email">
    </div>
    <div class="form-group">
      <label for="enterpassword" class="sr-only">Password</label>
      <input type="password" class="form-control"
      id="enterpassword" placeholder="Password">
    </div>
    <br><br>
    <div class="checkbox">
      <label> <input type="checkbox"> Keep me signed in </label>
    </div>
    <br><br>
    <div class="radio">
      <label>
        <input type="radio" name="optionsRadios" value="option1"
        id="radio1">
        Male
      </label>
    </div>

    <div class="radio">
      <label>
        <input type="radio" name="optionsRadios" value="option2"
        id="radio2">
        Female
      </label>
    </div>
    <br><br>
```

```
    <p> Enter your comments in the following box </p>
    <br>
    <textarea rows="5" cols="70" placeholder="Your feedback is
      important to us">
    </textarea>
    <br><br>
    <button type="submit" class="btn btn-default">Login</button>
  </form>
</body>
```

The output of the code on execution will be as follows:

If you observe the code and the preceding output, you can see that the inline style has been applied to the form as the two textboxes for the e-mail as well as the password are on a single line. You can also see that though we have defined the label for e-mail as well as the **Password** fields, they are hidden due to the definition of the sr-only class.

Screen readers will have trouble with your forms if you don't include a label for every input. For these inline forms, you can hide the labels using the sr-only class. You should always consider screen readers for accessibility purposes. Usage of the class will hide the element anyway, therefore, you shouldn't see a visual difference.

Horizontal forms

You can align the form labels and fields horizontally by adding the `form-horizontal` class to the form and using `div` elements with the Bootstrap Grid classes.

Take a look at the following code sample in the HTML document to understand it better:

```
<form class="form-horizontal" role="form">
  <div class="form-group" form-group-lg>
    <label for="Email_user" class="col-sm-2 control-
    label">Login</label>
    <div class="col-sm-4">
      <input type="email" class="form-control" id="Email_user"
      placeholder="Email OR Username">
    </div>
  </div>
  <div class="form-group" form-group-sm>
    <label for="inputPassword" class="col-sm-2 control-
    label">Password</label>
    <div class="col-sm-4">
      <input type="password" class="form-control"
      id="inputPassword" placeholder="Password">
    </div>
  </div>
  <div class="form-group">
    <div class="col-sm-offset-2 col-sm-4">
      <button type="submit" class="btn btn-primary"> Login
      </button>
    </div>
  </div>
</form>
```

The output of this code will be as follows:

As you can see, the form has a horizontal layout. You can also include block level help text by using the `help-block` class within the `<span>` element. You can also use optional icons in horizontal and inline forms using classes such as `has-success` and `has-feedback` to further enhance your forms.

Code

You can wrap inline code snippets using the `<code>` tag. However, for multiple blocks of code, we use the `<pre>` tag.

Take a look at the following code to help you understand it better:

```
<!DOCTYPE html>
<html>
<head>
  <title>Using the Bootstrap Grid classes</title>
  <meta name="viewport" content="width=device-width, initial-
  scale=1.0">
  <link href="css/bootstrap.css" rel="stylesheet" media="screen">
  <style>
    #packt {
      padding-top: 25px;
      padding-bottom: 25px;
      padding-right: 50px;
      padding-left: 50px;
    }
  </style>

</head>
<body id ="packt">
  <code>The &lt;p&gt; element</code>
  <pre>
    &lt;p class="text-left">Left aligned text.&lt;/p&gt;
    &lt;p class="text-center">Center aligned text.&lt;/p&gt;
    &lt;p class="text-right">Right aligned text.&lt;/p&gt;
    &lt;p&gt; Sample text here... &lt;/p&gt;
  </pre>
</body>
</html>
```

The output of this code will be as follows:

```
The <p> element

<p class="text-left">Left aligned text.</p>
<p class="text-center">Center aligned text.</p>
<p class="text-right">Right aligned text.</p>
<p> Sample text here... </p>
```

You have to use < and > for the angular brackets in the <code> tag.

Images

In Bootstrap, the <image> element is used to embed and style images in the document. You can also use the built-in classes to style the images with a rounded corner or a thumbnail.

Images can be made responsive using the img-responsive class. By this attribute, you can apply the maximum width of 100 percent and an automatic adjustment of height to the image, enabling it to scale easily with respect to the parent element.

Take a look at the following code to understand it better:

```
<!DOCTYPE html>
<html>
<head>
  <title>Images in Bootstrap</title>
  <meta name="viewport" content="width=device-width, initial-
  scale=1.0">
  <link href="css/bootstrap.css" rel="stylesheet" media="screen">
  <style>
    #packt {
      padding-top: 25px;
      padding-bottom: 25px;
      padding-right: 50px;
      padding-left: 50px;
    }
  </style>
</head>
<body id="packt">
```

```
<img src="packt_sample.png"    class="img-rounded" height="150"
width="130">
<br><br>
<img src="packt_sample.png"    class="img-circle">
<br><br>
<img src="packt_sample.png"    class="img-thumbnail"  height="75"
width="75">
</body>
</html>
```

The output of the code upon execution will be as follows:

Font families

Bootstrap includes defaults for sans-serif, serif, and monospace font families.

Sans-serif font family

The default sans-serif font family used in Bootstrap is `"Helvetica Neue"`, `Helvetica, Arial, sans-serif`. It can be changed with the LESS variable `@font-family-sans-serif`. It is also assigned to the LESS variable `@font-family-base`, which sets the base font family used by default everywhere in Bootstrap.

Serif font family

The default serif font family used in Bootstrap is `Georgia, "Times New Roman", Times, serif`. It is set in the LESS variable `@font-family-serif`.

The serif font family is not used by default but you can use the LESS variable `@font-family-serif` or you can assign it to the LESS variable `@font-family-base` so that it replaces the sans-serif font everywhere.

Monospace font family

The font family used for monospace text—`<code>` and `<pre>` HTML tags—is `Monaco, Menlo, Consolas, "Courier New", monospace`. The corresponding LESS variable is `@font-family-monospace`.

Font sizes

The default font sizes of HTML elements provided by Bootstrap are consistent and can be quickly adapted to your use cases by modifying LESS variables.

Font sizes variables

Bootstrap has various LESS variables to customize the font sizes:

- `@font-size-base`: This is the base font size used across Bootstrap. By default, all paragraphs use this font size. Other HTML elements such as lists and code also use it. The value of `@font-size-base` is 14 px by default. You can change it by adding a line like the following in your custom LESS style sheet.

- `@font-size-base: 16px`: The HTML elements such as headings and blockquotes don't use the base font size; instead they use a font size which is a multiple of the base font size. Changing the base font size will also change the font sizes of these HTML elements. This ensures consistency across your website design so that you don't end up with elements that are not adequately proportional with each other.

- `@font-size-large`: This is the font size used for large buttons and form fields, large paginations and the brand name in the navigation bar. The default value is 18 px, which is approximately 1.25 times the base font size of 14 px.

- `@font-size-small`: This is the font size used for small buttons and form fields, small paginations, badges, and progress bars. The default value is 12 px, which is approximately 0.85 times the base font size of 14 px.

Font sizes for headings

Font size for headings can also be manipulated by assigning a different value to the headings using the following code in the custom LESS file. The default font sizes for the headings are as follows:

- `@font-size-h1: 36px;`

- `@font-size-h2: 30px;`

- `@font-size-h3: 24px;`

- `@font-size-h4: 18px;`

- `@font-size-h5: 14px;`

- `@font-size-h6: 12px;`

By altering the values in your custom LESS file, you can change the size of the variables.

Customizing the Base CSS using LESS variables

Bootstrap has LESS variables that can be used for components and the default values are listed as follows:

```
@padding-base-vertical:      6px;
@padding-base-horizontal:    12px;

@padding-large-vertical:     10px;
@padding-large-horizontal:   16px;

@padding-small-vertical:     5px;
@padding-small-horizontal:   10px;

@padding-xs-vertical:        1px;
@padding-xs-horizontal:      5px;

@line-height-large:          1.33;
@line-height-small:          1.5;

@border-radius-base:         4px;
@border-radius-large:        6px;
@border-radius-small:        3px;
```

```
@component-active-color:    #fff;
@component-active-bg:    @brand-primary;

@caret-width-base:            4px;
@caret-width-large:           5px;
```

You can change the `placeholder` contextual color using the following code:

```
.placeholder(@color: @input-color-placeholder) {
  &::-moz-placeholder              { color: @color; } // Firefox
  &:-ms-input-placeholder          { color: @color; } // Internet
  Explorer 10+
  &::-webkit-input-placeholder   { color: @color; } // Safari and
  Chrome
}
```

Bootstrap uses `@body-bg: #fff;` and `@text-color: @black-50;` for the body background and the text color. You can alter the background or text color by assigning different values for the background color and text color.

You can style your links with your preferred choice by assigning values to the following fields:

```
@link-color:         @brand-primary;
@link-hover-color: darken(@link-color, 15%);
```

We will take a look at the following code to help you understand how we can customize the Base CSS using LESS variables:

```
<!DOCTYPE html>
<html>
<head>
  <title> Base Css with LESS </title>
  <meta name="viewport" content="width=device-width, initial-
  scale=1.0">
  <link href="css/bootstrap.css" rel="stylesheet" media="screen">
  <style>
    #packt {
      padding-top: 25px;
      padding-bottom: 25px;
      padding-right: 50px;
```

```
      padding-left: 50px;
    }
    hr { background-color: red; height: 1px; border: 0; }
  </style>
  <link href="css/style.css" rel="stylesheet" media="screen">
</head>
<body id="packt">
  <h1> Manipulating Bootstrap Base Css with LESS </h1>
  <hr>
    <h6> Packt Publishing </h2>
    <p>Packt's mission is to help the world put software to work
    in new ways.</p>
  <hr>
  <form role="form">
    <div class="form-group">
      <label for="enterusername"> Enter Email Address as the
      Username</label>
      <input type="email" class="form-control"
      id="enterusername" placeholder="Enter email">
    </div>
    <div class="form-group">
      <label for="enterpassword">Password</label>
      <input type="password" class="form-control"
      id="enterpassword" placeholder="Password">
    </div>
    <br>
    <div class="form-group">
      <label for="filebrowse">Browse to find file</label>
      <input type="file" id="filebrowse">
    </div>
    <br><br>

    <button type="submit" class="btn btn-
    primary">Login</button>
  </form>
</body>
</html>
```

The output of the code will be as follows:

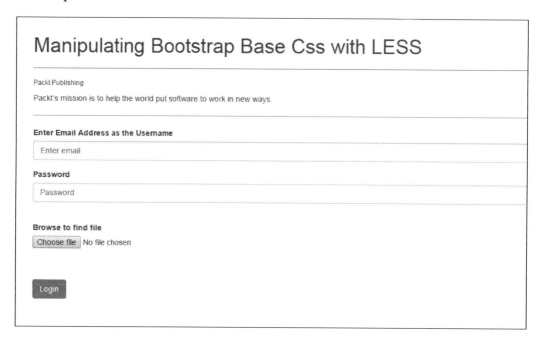

As you can see from the preceding code and output, we have not yet defined the `style.less` file.

First, copy and paste the `less` files from the source code into a file called `bootstrap` in the `css` folder similar to what we did in *Chapter 3, Using the Bootstrap Grid*. Then create a `style.less` file in the `css` folder and copy the following code into the `style.less` file:

```
@import "bootstrap/bootstrap.less";
@font-size-base: 15px;
@font-size-h1: 20px;
@font-size-h6: 45px;
@body-bg: #996600;
@input-bg: #FFFF99;
@btn-primary-color: #00FF33;
@btn-primary-bg: #660000;
```

In the code, we have changed the value of font-size-base to 15px. The font size of headings <h1> and <h6> have been changed to 20px and 45px respectively. The body background color was changed to #996600 and the input form field color was changed to #FFFF99. Finally, we changed the color of the primary button to #00FF33 and the background color of the primary button to #660000. Save the file and covert the style.less file to style.css using the SimpLESS or WinLess compiler.

Upon execution, we will get the following screen with all the changes incorporated:

From the preceding code and output, you can see that the Bootstrap styles and the padding styles have been overridden with the style.css file resulting in a different output. Thus, you can modify most of the Base CSS styles using LESS variables.

Summary

In this chapter, you learned about the Base CSS styles offered by Bootstrap. You also learned about different types of typographic elements, emphasis classes and emphasis elements, forms, tables, and buttons to mention a few. Finally, you learned how to customize Base CSS with the help of LESS variables.

In the next chapter, we will look at some of the popular CSS components included by Bootstrap and how to use them in your project, thereby enabling you to build a website with ease.

5
Adding Bootstrap Components

The Grid and the Base CSS constitute the rock-solid foundation of Bootstrap. Components are an imperative cog in the wheel in web designing with Bootstrap. They are single fragments of markup, sometimes bound to JavaScript functionalities, ready to be chosen, copied, and used in our web pages.

Terms such as **modularity, code reusability,** and **separation of responsibilities** are consistently linked to web development. These attributes lead to easy code maintenance, readability, and save the developers a lot of time and effort, resulting in a systematic and organized approach.

In this chapter, we'll take a look at the following Bootstrap components:

- Glyphicons
- Navs
- Nav tabs
- Nav pills
- Navbars
- Dropdowns
- Breadcrumbs

Components and their usage

In Bootstrap, a component may be used regardless of the other components and its default style is already defined inside the main Bootstrap CSS (though a few may also require JavaScript). Thus, you can generate as many different instances of a component as per your requirements with the same visual style applied to them and saving yourself precious time and effort, thereby allowing you to focus on the more vital parts of your development process.

Glyphicons

Glyphicons is a utility of monochromatic icons and symbols with emphasis on simplicity, keeping usability in mind. The creators of Glyphicons have provided these icons free of cost for Bootstrap. The official Glyphicons web page at `http://glyphicons.com/` contains a detailed list of all the icons that are of great use while developing complex websites, as icons are better than words in most cases.

The following screenshot displays some of the popular Glyphicons available for Bootstrap:

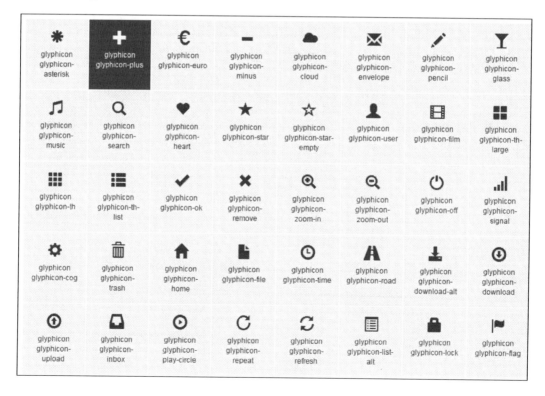

Take a look at the following code to understand it better:

```html
<!DOCTYPE html>
<html>
<head>
<title> Bootstrap 3 Glyphicons</title>
<link rel="stylesheet" href="http://maxcdn.bootstrapcdn.com/
bootstrap/3.2.0/css/bootstrap.min.css">
<link rel="stylesheet" href="http://maxcdn.bootstrapcdn.com/
bootstrap/3.2.0/css/bootstrap-theme.min.css">
<script src="http://ajax.googleapis.com/ajax/libs/jquery/1.11.1/
jquery.min.js"></script>
<script src="http://maxcdn.bootstrapcdn.com/bootstrap/3.2.0/js/
bootstrap.min.js"></script>
<style type="text/css">
    #pub {
       padding: 50px 100px 50px 50px;;
    }
   #packt{
    float:right;
    display:block;
    margin-right:0px;
    clear:left;
}
    #packtpub{
    float:right;
    display:block;
    margin-right:0px;
    clear:left;
}
</style>
</head>
<body>
<div id="pub">
    <form>
        <div class="row">
            <div class="col-xs-7">
                <div class="input-group">
                    <span class="input-group-addon"><span
class="glyphicon glyphicon-search"></span></span>
                    <input type="text" class="form-control"
placeholder="Search ">
                </div>
                </div>
        <br><br>
```

```
            <button type="submit" class="btn btn-success"
id="packt"><span class="glyphicon glyphicon-log-in"></span> Login </
button>
        <br>
        <br>
        <button type="submit" class="btn btn-default"><span
class="glyphicon glyphicon-envelope"></span> Mail</button>
        <br>
        <br>
        <button type="submit" class="btn btn-default"><span
class="glyphicon glyphicon-user"></span> Find Friends </button>
        <br>
        <br>
        <button type="submit" class="btn btn-warning"><span
class="glyphicon glyphicon-trash"></span> Empty Trash </button>
        <br><br><br>
        <p> To get rid of malware, Click on the following button </p>
        <button type="submit" class="btn btn-danger"><span
class="glyphicon glyphicon-log-out"></span> Clean System</button>
            <br><br>
             <button type="submit" class="btn btn-success"
id="packtpub"><span class="glyphicon glyphicon-log-out"></span> Log
out</button>
        </div>
</form>
</div>
</body>
</html>
```

The output of this code upon execution will be as follows:

In the `<head>` section, we've included Bootstrap files such as the Bootstrap JavaScript file and the Bootstrap theme CSS file in addition to styling with custom CSS. We've defined the search icon by including the `<span class="glyphicon glyphicon-search"></span>` code. Similarly, we've added the **Login** icon by using the `<span class="glyphicon glyphicon-log-in"></span>` code. Thus, all the icons need a base class along with the individual icon class. However, one point to note is that the icon classes cannot be directly combined with other components, nor can they be used alongside other classes on the same element. Hence a nested `<span>` tag is used for inline elements whereas the Glyphicons have to be defined as the class for that `<span>` tag.

In all the code examples, we may use padding or a margin so that the output is not too close to the left of the view, thereby helping us take screenshots easily in addition to improving the aesthetics of our design.

Nav tabs

The nav component generates beautiful navigation elements by decorating lists. In HTML, a list is a nestable element used to specify varied information in an ordered (`<ol>`) or unordered (`<ul>`) manner. Depending on whether it is ordered or unordered, it is presented as enumerated or by *de facto* bullet points. Using Bootstrap, you can remove the default browser list style and make every link appear as a block.

Take a look at the following code to understand this better:

```
<!DOCTYPE html>
<html>
<head>
<title>Bootstrap Nav and Nav Tabs</title>
<link rel="stylesheet" href="http://maxcdn.bootstrapcdn.com/
bootstrap/3.2.0/css/bootstrap.min.css">
<link rel="stylesheet" href="http://maxcdn.bootstrapcdn.com/
bootstrap/3.2.0/css/bootstrap-theme.min.css">
<script src="http://ajax.googleapis.com/ajax/libs/jquery/1.11.1/
jquery.min.js"></script>
<script src="http://maxcdn.bootstrapcdn.com/bootstrap/3.2.0/js/
bootstrap.min.js"></script>
<style type="text/css">
    .packt{
      margin: 25px 50px 75px 100px;
    }
</style>
</head>
```

```
<body>
<div class="packt">
  <ul class="nav">
        <li class="active"><a href="#"> <span class="glyphicon
glyphicon-sd-video"> </span> Videos</a></li>
        <li><a href="#"> <span class="glyphicon glyphicon-book"> </
span> Books</a></li>
        <li><a href="#"> <span class="glyphicon glyphicon-inbox"> </
span> Inbox</a></li>
  </ul>
</div>
</body>
</html>
```

The output of this code will be as follows:

You will see that the <nav> element removes the list style. We have also added
Glyphicons to each link in the list for enhanced effects.

Now let's add the .nav-tabs class in conjunction with the .nav class.
Therefore, the changed code snippet is as follows:

```
<ul class="nav nav-tabs">
        <li class="active"><a href="#"> <span class="glyphicon
glyphicon-sd-video"> </span> Videos</a></li>
        <li><a href="#"> <span class="glyphicon glyphicon-book"> </
span> Books</a></li>
        <li><a href="#"> <span class="glyphicon glyphicon-inbox"> </
span> Inbox</a></li>
  </ul>
```

The output of this code upon execution will be as follows:

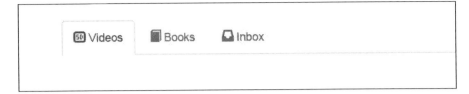

From the output, you can see that up on adding `.nav-tabs`, the menu items are displayed as tabs and positioned next to each other instead of being vertically stacked. Moreover, the item width is based on the text length.

Nav pills

In order to get a pill-based navigation, you need to replace `.nav-tabs` with `.nav-pills`.

 Pills can be links or buttons that are arranged horizontally and are drawn with a visual style that indicate an association between them.

Take a look at the following code snippet to understand this better:

```
<div class="packt">
  <ul class="nav nav-pills">
        <li class="active"><a href="#"> <span class="glyphicon
glyphicon-sd-video"> </span> Videos</a></li>
        <li><a href="#"> <span class="glyphicon glyphicon-book"> </
span> Books</a></li>
        <li><a href="#"> <span class="glyphicon glyphicon-inbox"> </
span> Inbox</a></li>
  </ul>
</div>
```

The output of this code will be as follows:

Let's add the `.nav-stacked` class to the `.nav-pills` class using the following line of code:

```
<ul class="nav nav-pills nav-stacked">
```

The output of this code upon execution will be as follows:

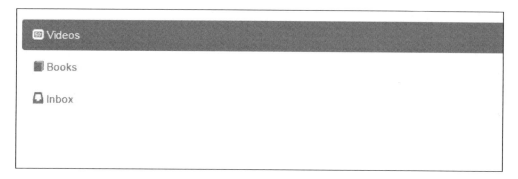

As you can see from the output, the pills are now vertically stacked.

Justified tabs and pills

In order to make the width of your tabs and pills the same as that of the parent element, you can add an extra class, `.nav-justified`. However, in screens smaller than 768 pixels, the navigation links will be stacked.

Take a look at the following code snippet to understand this better:

```
<body>
<div class="packt">
<h3> Justified tabs for Nav-Tabs </h3>
  <ul class="nav nav-tabs nav-justified">
  <li class="active"><a href="#">Guitar</a></li>
        <li><a href="#">Violin</a></li>
        <li><a href="#">Saxophone</a></li>
  <li class="disabled"><a href="#">Harp</a></li>
      </ul>
  <br><hr><br>
<h3> Justified tabs for Nav-Pills </h3>
      <ul class="nav nav-pills nav-justified">
        <li class="active"><a href="#">Guitar</a></li>
        <li><a href="#">Violin</a></li>
        <li><a href="#">Saxophone</a></li>
  <li class="disabled"><a href="#">Harp</a></li>
      </ul>
</div>
</body>
```

The output of this code will be as follows:

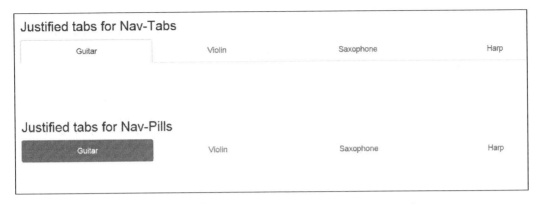

Therefore, from the output, you can see that the tabs and pills have an equal width of the parent element.

Dropdowns

If there are several links on a page, it becomes too big and cluttered. An effective way to avoid this is to use a drop-down menu so that you can include as many links as possible using a small percentage of the screen.

You can add drop-down menus for buttons, tab, pills, and navbar to mention a few. In the following code example, we'll create a drop-down menu for `.nav-tabs`:

```html
<!DOCTYPE html>
<html>
<head>
<title> Dropdowns in Bootstrap 3 </title>
<link rel="stylesheet" href="http://maxcdn.bootstrapcdn.com/
bootstrap/3.2.0/css/bootstrap.min.css">
<link rel="stylesheet" href="http://maxcdn.bootstrapcdn.com/
bootstrap/3.2.0/css/bootstrap-theme.min.css">
<script src="http://ajax.googleapis.com/ajax/libs/jquery/1.11.1/
jquery.min.js"></script>
<script src="http://maxcdn.bootstrapcdn.com/bootstrap/3.2.0/js/
bootstrap.min.js"></script>
<style type="text/css">
    #packt{
      padding: 30px;
    }
</style>
</head>
```

```
<body id="packt">
<div>
    <ul class="nav nav-tabs">
        <li class="active"><a href="#"> <span class="glyphicon
glyphicon-home"> </span> Packt Home Page</a></li>
        <li><a href="#"> <span class="glyphicon glyphicon-user"> </
span> Authors</a></li>
        <li class="dropdown">
            <a href="#" data-toggle="dropdown" class="dropdown-
toggle"> Blogs <b class="caret"></b></a>
            <ul class="dropdown-menu">
                <li><a href="https://www.packtpub.com/books/content/
blogs"><span class="glyphicon glyphicon-book">

</span> Blog </a></li>
                <li><a href="https://www.packtpub.com/books/content/
tech-hub"><span class="glyphicon glyphicon-

bookmark"> </span> Tech Hub </a></li>
                <li><a href="https://www.packtpub.com/books/content/
article-network"><span class="
glyphicon glyphicon-book"> </span> Article Network </a></li>
                <li class="divider"></li>
                <li><a href="https://www.packtpub.com/books/content/
support">Support</a></li>
            </ul>
        </li>
    </ul>
</div>
</body>
</html>
```

The output of this code upon on execution will be as follows:

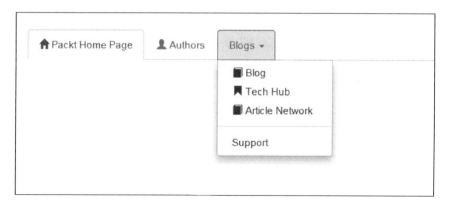

If you observe the code and the subsequent output, we created navigation tabs and defined the list of items in addition to using Glyphicons with the list. Now, we assign a drop-down class and add the drop-down toggle for the `anchor` tag and create a caret in addition to defining the drop-down functionality using the `data-toggle="dropdown"` attribute. After the **Blog, Tech Hub,** and **Article Network** items were created in the list, we defined a `.divider` class, which will split the drop-down menu. Later on, we defined the **Support** item in the list. On clicking the **Blogs** tab, we can see that the drop-down menu has been created and there is a divider separating the first three items and the **Support** item.

This process can also be used for `.nav-pills` and buttons too. It can also be applied to the navbar, which we will see in the next example.

Navbar

The navbar component gives you the power to generate portions of self-contained bars, which could be used as whole-application headers, versatile secondary menus for page content, or as a shell of various navigation-related elements. You can develop static navbars with simple navigations or navbars with forms, search boxes, and drop-down menus too.

Take a look at the following code to understand this better:

```
<!DOCTYPE html>
<html>
<head>
<title> Boostrap NavBar </title>
<link rel="stylesheet" href="http://maxcdn.bootstrapcdn.com/
bootstrap/3.2.0/css/bootstrap.min.css">
<link rel="stylesheet" href="http://maxcdn.bootstrapcdn.com/
bootstrap/3.2.0/css/bootstrap-theme.min.css">
<script src="http://ajax.googleapis.com/ajax/libs/jquery/1.11.1/
jquery.min.js"></script>
<script src="http://maxcdn.bootstrapcdn.com/bootstrap/3.2.0/js/
bootstrap.min.js"></script>
<style type="text/css">
    .packt{
      padding: 30px;
    }
</style>
</head>
<body class="packt">
<div>
    <nav role="navigation" class="navbar navbar-default">
        <div class="navbar-header">
```

```html
                    <button type="button" data-target="#navbarCollapse" data-
toggle="collapse" class="navbar-toggle">
                        <span class="sr-only">Toggle navigation</span>
                        <span class="icon-bar"></span>
                        <span class="icon-bar"></span>
                        <span class="icon-bar"></span>
                    </button>
                    <a href="#" class="navbar-brand">Packt Publishing</a>
                </div>
                <div id="navbarCollapse" class="collapse navbar-collapse">
                    <ul class="nav navbar-nav">
                        <li class="active"><a href="#"> Books and Videos </
a></li>
                        <li><a href="#"> Articles </a></li>
                        <li class="dropdown">
                            <a data-toggle="dropdown" class="dropdown-toggle"
href="#"> Categories <b class="caret"></b></a>
                            <ul role="menu" class="dropdown-menu">
                                <li><a href="#"> Web development </a></li>
                                <li><a href="#"> Game Development </a></li>
                                <li><a href="#"> Big Data and Business
Intelligence </a></li>
                                <li><a href="#"> Virtualization and Cloud </a></
li>
                                <li><a href="#"> Networking and Servers </a></li>
                                <li class="divider"></li>
                                <li><a href="#"> Miscellaneous </a></li>
                            </ul>
                        </li>
            <li><a href="#"> Support </a></li>
                    </ul>
                    <form role="search" class="navbar-form navbar-right">
                        <div class="form-group">
                            <input type="text" placeholder="Search Here"
class="form-control">
                        </div>
                    </form>
                </div>
            </nav>
        </div>
    </body>
</html>
```

The output of this code will be as follows:

In the preceding code, you can see the navbar in action. Let's discuss the code so that you can understand the reason for its output.

To create a navbar, you need to define the role as `navigation` and use the `.navbar navbar-default` class. Then, we define the `.navbar-header` class and later on define a button. The button element has an ID defined for its data target value which you can use to dynamically hide or show the element. Then the `.collapse` functionality is defined and uses the JavaScript file of Bootstrap.

 The `sr-only` helper class should be used in those cases where the inner text has to be available for screen readers, bots, and crawlers but must remain invisible for the users of your website.

Next, we assign the value `Packt Publishing` to the anchor link containing the `.navbar-brand` class. Then we create navigation tabs using the `.navbar-nav` class, and create the navigation tabs for the navbar in the same way as we created the tabs using the `.nav-tabs` class. Finally, we create a basic form with the search function by defining the `<form>` element and the `.navbar-form` class. In addition to this, we shift the search box to the right using the `.navbar-right` class.

By adding `.navbar-fixed-top` in addition to the `.navbar` and `.navbar-default` base class, you can create a navbar that is fixed at the top. However, you need to include a `.container` class or a `.container-fluid` class along with it to center and pad the navbar content. The code snippet has to be defined in the following manner:

```
<nav role="navigation" class="navbar navbar-default navbar-fixed-top">
    <div class="container-fluid">
```

Similarly, you can use the `.navbar-fixed-bottom` class to create navbars fixed to the bottom. Using the fixed top and bottom class attributes, you can create a navbar that remains visible and scrolls with the page content.

Remember to define the `padding-top` style in the CSS to the body element, which must be equal or greater than the navbar height so that the page content is not overlapped.

If you want a fixed top navbar without any padding, you can alternatively use the `.navbar-static-top` class in conjunction with the `.navbar` and `.navbar-default` class:

```
<nav role="navigation" class="navbar navbar-default navbar-static-
top">
    <div class="container-fluid">
```

Remember that you also need to define the `.container` class or the `.container-fluid` class like the top and bottom fixed navbar scenarios.

Breadcrumbs

Breadcrumbs are used to enhance the accessibility of your websites by indicating the location using a navigational hierarchy, especially in websites with a significant number of web pages.

Take a look at the following code to understand this better:

```
<!DOCTYPE html>
<html>
<head>
<title>Bootstrap 3 Breadcrumbs</title>
<link rel="stylesheet" href="http://maxcdn.bootstrapcdn.com/
bootstrap/3.2.0/css/bootstrap.min.css">
<link rel="stylesheet" href="http://maxcdn.bootstrapcdn.com/
bootstrap/3.2.0/css/bootstrap-theme.min.css">
<script src="http://ajax.googleapis.com/ajax/libs/jquery/1.11.1/
jquery.min.js"></script>
<script src="http://maxcdn.bootstrapcdn.com/bootstrap/3.2.0/js/
bootstrap.min.js"></script>
<style type="text/css">
    #packt, h1{
      margin: 20px;
        padding: 15px;
    }
</style>
```

```
</head>
<body>
<h1> BreadCrumbs in Bootstrap </h1>
<div id="packt">
    <ul class="breadcrumb">
        <li><a href="#">Tech Hub</a></li>
        <li><a href="#">Blogs</a></li>
        <li class="active">Article Network</li>
        <li><a href="#">Books and Videos</a></li>
        <li><a href="#">Support</a></li>
    </ul>
</div>
</body>
</html>
```

The output of this code upon execution will be as follows:

BreadCrumbs in Bootstrap

Tech Hub / Blogs / Article Network / Books and Videos / Support

As you can see from the output, it helps you to depict your location in the web page or web application. We have assigned the `.active` class for the **Article Network** list item to give it a real world look.

Summary

In this chapter, we discussed the widely-used components, specifically the navigation-based ones. We also had a look at the `Dropdown` component and the Glyphicons used in Bootstrap 3.2.

In the next chapter, you will learn about the remaining components such as `Alerts`, `Button-Groups`, `badges`, `labels`, `pagination`, and `panels` to name a few.

6
Doing More with Components

In the previous chapter, we looked at the navigation components, dropdowns, and the Glyphicons that are widely used to create a website with Bootstrap. In this chapter, we will take a look at the remaining components which make web designing very easy.

The following components will be covered in this chapter:

- Jumbotron
- Page header
- Wells
- Badges
- Labels
- Progress bars
- Panels
- Thumbnails
- List groups
- Button groups and group sizes
- The Button toolbar
- Checkbox and radio button groups
- Alerts
- Pagination and pager
- Media objects and the responsive embed attribute

Components to streamline your web designing projects

We will now look at the components that aid in code reusability, thereby adhering to the **Don't Repeat Yourself (DRY)** principle, meaning that these modules can be included in the code. This results in saving time and effort, thereby allowing you to focus on the more imperative things in your projects.

The following code snippet will be used in almost all the code examples:

```html
<!DOCTYPE html>
<html>
<head>
<title>Page Header Segmentation</title>
<link rel="stylesheet" href="http://maxcdn.bootstrapcdn.com/
bootstrap/3.2.0/css/bootstrap.min.css">
<link rel="stylesheet" href="http://maxcdn.bootstrapcdn.com/
bootstrap/3.2.0/css/bootstrap-theme.min.css">
<script src="http://ajax.googleapis.com/ajax/libs/jquery/1.11.1/
jquery.min.js"></script>
<script src="http://maxcdn.bootstrapcdn.com/bootstrap/3.2.0/js/
bootstrap.min.js"></script>
<style type="text/css">
      #packtpub{
      padding-top: 30px;
    padding-right: 50px;
    padding-left: 50px;
            }
</style>
</head>
```

In the preceding code, we defined the required Bootstrap files including the jQuery and the Bootstrap JavaScript file in the `<head>` section. We also used padding or margins defined in the `<style>` tags for aesthetic purposes. Hence, we will only see the main code snippet in all the examples in this chapter so that you do not get overwhelmed with coding. Please refer to the code bundle for the entire code.

Jumbotron

Using the **Jumbotron** component, you can emphasize the key content on your website. Important information can be showcased in addition to increasing the aesthetics of the web page.

Look at the following code to understand this better:

```
<!DOCTYPE html>
<html>
<head>
<title>Full width JumboTron</title>
<link rel="stylesheet" href="http://maxcdn.bootstrapcdn.com/
bootstrap/3.2.0/css/bootstrap.min.css">
<link rel="stylesheet" href="http://maxcdn.bootstrapcdn.com/
bootstrap/3.2.0/css/bootstrap-theme.min.css">
<script src="http://ajax.googleapis.com/ajax/libs/jquery/1.11.1/
jquery.min.js"></script>
<script src="http://maxcdn.bootstrapcdn.com/bootstrap/3.2.0/js/
bootstrap.min.js"></script>
<style type="text/css">
    .jumbotron{
      margin-top: 15px;
  padding: 17px;
  color: #990000;
background-color: #FFFFCC;
      }
</style>
</head>
<body>
<div class="jumbotron">
   <div class="container">
       <h1> Packt Publishing </h1>
       <p>Packt is committed to bringing you relevant learning
resources for the latest tools and technologies. At <a href="https://
www.packtpub.com/" >Packt</a>, our mission is to help the world put
software to work in new ways, through the delivery of effective
learning and information services to IT professionals</p>
<p><a href="https://www.packtpub.com/all" target="_blank" class="btn
btn-primary btn-lg"> Books and Videos </a></p>
   </div>
</div>
</body>
</html>
```

The output of the preceding code will be as follows:

As you can see, **Packt Publishing** and the content relevant to it is emphasized, allocating extra attention to it. We also applied styles to the Jumbotron component by introducing the padding and margin in addition to defining the text as well as the background color. It is a good practice to include the Jumbotron component followed by a `container` element to remove rounded corners and cover the full width of the viewport.

Page header

The page header component is used to introduce space as well as segment sections of the featured content. It is generally used with the *heading 1* (`<h1>`) element and extends support to `<small>` and other elements making it a useful utility in your web design.

Look at the following code snippet to understand this better:

```
<body id="packtpub">
<div  class="page-header">
    <h1>Packt Publishing: <small>Always finding a way</small></h1>
</div>
</body>
```

The output of this code will be as follows:

If you observe the output, you can clearly see the segmentation for the <h1> as well as its <small> default element.

Wells

The well component is used to give an inset effect to the content. Look at the following code to understand it better:

```
<body id="packt">
    <h3><u> Using wells for an inset effect </u></h3>
  <br><hr>
<div>
    <div class="well"> I formulate infinity </div>
    <div class="well well-lg"> I formulate infinity </div>
    <div class="well well-sm"> I formulate infinity </div>
</div>
</body>
```

The output of this code upon execution will be as follows:

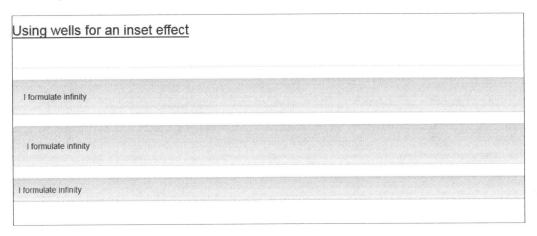

In this code, we defined the size of the well component by defining well-lg and well-sm for the second and third well component resulting in large and small sizes, apart from the default .well class. The .well-lg and .well-sm classes are modifier classes which can be used to control padding and the rounded corners.

Badges

Badges are used for notifications, which indicate things such as unread messages, any new information, and number of e-mails still in the folder. Badges are commonly used in social networking websites, which help the users to know the latest information and updates.

Here is an example code explaining the use of badges to help you understand it better:

```
<body>
<div id="packt">
    <ul class="nav nav-tabs">
        <li><a href="#"> Settings</a></li>
        <li><a href="#"> Contacts</a></li>
        <li><a href="#"> Notifications <span class="badge">19</span></
a></li>
        <li class="active"><a href="#">Inbox <span class="badge">50</
span></a></li>
    </ul>
</div>
</body>
```

The output of this code upon execution be as follows:

From this code and output, you can observe that we have defined the badges for **Notifications** and **Inbox**. Badges can be used on various occasions such as links, nav tabs, and nav pills. In the preceding example, we used badges with nav-tabs.

Labels

Labels are used to depict essential information, which is quite significant and crucial to understand, such as important messages and notes. We can also use contextual colors to further highlight them.

Look at the following code to understand this better:

```
<body>
<div id="packt">
    <h1>Packt Publishing<span class="label label-default"> Deal of the
Day </span></h1>
    <h2>Packt Publishing<span class="label label-default"> The Packt
guarantee</span></h2>
    <h3>Packt Publishing <span class="label label-default"> Packt
Bonanza</span></h3>
    <p>Packt<span class="label label-primary"> Always finding a way</
span></p>
    <p>Packt<span class="label label-success"> Online Subscription
Service</span></p>
    <p>Packt<span class="label label-info"> PacktLib: the Online
library</span></p>
</div>
</body>
```

The output of the code will be as follows:

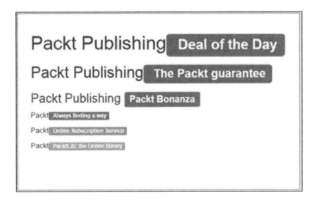

In this code, we defined the default, primary, success, and information context to the labels resulting in the preceding output.

Progress bars

Progress bars are used to show the status of the workflow or action, thereby helping you to determine the stage of execution. These are widely used, as they indicate the progress of the implemented workflow.

Look at the following code to understand them better:

```
<body id="packt">
    <div class="progress progress-striped active">
        <div class="progress-bar" style="width: 70%;">
            <span class="sr-only">70% Complete</span>
        </div>
    </div>
</body>
```

The output of this code will be as follows:

In the code, we included the .progress-striped and .active classes to the .progress class. If we only use the .progress class, then we would end up with a solid bar denoting the progress. However, by defining the .progress-striped class along with the .active class, the solid bar turns into a striped gradient, whereas the .active class depicts the animation giving it a real-time scenario look.

We can also add contextual alternatives to the progress bar. Look at this example to understand it better:

```
<body>
<div class="packt">
  <div class="progress progress-striped active">
    <div class="progress-bar progress-bar-success"  style="width:
50%">
        <span class="sr-only">50% Complete (success)</span>
    </div>
    <div class="progress-bar progress-bar-info" style="width: 30%">
      <span class="sr-only">30% Complete (Info)</span>
    </div>
    <div class="progress-bar progress-bar-warning" style="width: 10%">
      <span class="sr-only">10% Complete (Warning)</span>
    </div>
  </div>
</div>
</body>
```

The output of the preceding code will be as follows:

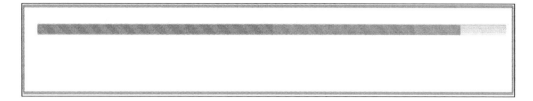

As you can clearly see, the preceding output depicts the various stages of progress with the contextual colors enhancing and defining the workflow action status.

Panels

Panels are used to place content in a box. Things such as tips and information boxes on a website can be assigned the panel class to display such information.

Take a look at the following code to help you understand this better:

```
<body>
<div id="packt"">
    <div class="panel panel-default">
        <div class="panel-heading">Packt Publishing </div>
<div class="panel-body"><a href="https://www.packtpub.
com/"><strong>Click here</strong></a> to go to the official webpage</
div>
    </div>
</div>
</body>
```

The output of the code will be as follows:

> Packt Publishing
>
> Click here to go to the official webpage

In the preceding code, we defined the `panel` class and assigned the default attribute to it. We also defined a `.panel-heading` class for the panel to add a heading container to the panel. In the output, you can see that the information displayed in a box has **Packt Publishing** as its heading.

 You can also use the `.panel-footer` class for secondary text, but you need to remember that panel footers don't inherit colors and borders even if you use contextual colors for it.

We can also use panels along with tables to make it informative for the website users, including adding contextual colors to it to convey the relevant semantics.

Look at the following code to understand this better:

```
<body>
<div id="packt">

            <div class="panel panel-success">
        <div class="panel-heading">
            <h3 class="panel-title">Panels with Tables</h3>
  </div>
  <div class="panel-body">
  <p> Following is a description of varied roles that people play. </
p>
    </div>

  <!-- Table -->
  <table class="table">
    <thead>
      <tr>

        <th>Name</th>
        <th>Nickname</th>
        <th>Profession</th>
      </tr>
    </thead>
    <tbody>
      <tr>

        <td>Aravind Shenoy</td>
        <td>Al</td>
        <td>Technical Content Writer</td>
      </tr>
      <tr>
```

```
            <td>James Douglas Morrison</td>
            <td>Jim</td>
            <td>Amazing Vocalist</td>
          </tr>
          <tr>

            <td>James Marshall Hendrix</td>
            <td>Jimi</td>
            <td>Awesome Guitarist</td>
          </tr>
        </tbody>
      </table>
    </div>
    </div>
  </div>
  </body>
```

The output of this code will be as follows:

Panels with Tables		
Following is a description of varied roles that people play.		
Name	**Nickname**	**Profession**
Aravind Shenoy	Al	Technical Content Writer
James Douglas Morrison	Jim	Amazing Vocalist
James Marshall Hendrix	Jimi	Awesome Guitarist

Apart from the defined contextual color for panels in the preceding code, you can alternatively use `.panel-primary`, `.panel-info`, `.panel-warning`, and `.panel-danger` as per your requirement.

Thumbnails

Thumbnails in Bootstrap can be customized to add HTML content and showcase buttons and paragraphs along with the linked images.

Look at the following code to understand this better:

```
<body id="packtpub">
<div class="row">
  <div class="col-sm-6 col-md-4">
```

```
<div class="thumbnail">
   <img src="Angular.png" height="133" width="133" alt="AngularJS">
   <div class="caption">
     <h3>AngularJS</h3>
     <p>Streamline your web applications with this hands-on course.
From initial structuring to full deployment, you'll learn everything
you need to know about AngularJS DOM based frameworks.</p>
       <p><a href="#" class="btn btn-primary" role="button"> E-book</
a><a href="#" class="btn btn-default" role="button">Print + Ebook </
a></p>
     </div>
   </div>
 </div>
</div>
</body>
```

The output of the preceding code will be as follows:

As you can clearly see, the heading, paragraph, and buttons are showcased alongside the thumbnail image. You can also add a caption to it. This kind of attribute is quite useful in shopping portals as you have relevant information related to the showcased products next to the thumbnail.

Pagination

You may have come across the number of pages when you use the search feature to look for some information. Pagination helps you do just that by creating a number of pages for search results for some topic, blog, or forum.

Take a look at the following code example to understand it better:

```
<body id="packt">
<div>
  <div>
      <ul class="pagination pagination-lg">
          <li class="disabled"><span>&laquo;</span></li>
          <li class="active"><a href="#">1</a></li>
          <li><a href="#">2</a></li>
          <li><a href="#">3</a></li>
          <li><a href="#">4</a></li>
          <li><a href="#">5</a></li>
          <li><a href="#">&raquo;</a></li>
      </ul>
  </div>
  <div>
      <ul class="pagination">
          <li class="disabled"><span>&laquo;</span></li>
          <li class="active"><a href="#">1</a></li>
          <li><a href="#">2</a></li>
          <li><a href="#">3</a></li>
          <li><a href="#">4</a></li>
          <li><a href="#">5</a></li>
          <li><a href="#">&raquo;</a></li>
      </ul>
  </div>
  <div>
      <ul class="pagination pagination-sm">
          <li class="disabled"><span>&laquo;</span></li>
          <li class="active"><a href="#">1</a></li>
          <li><a href="#">2</a></li>
          <li><a href="#">3</a></li>
          <li><a href="#">4</a></li>
          <li><a href="#">5</a></li>
          <li><a href="#">&raquo;</a></li>
      </ul>
  </div>
</div>
</body>
```

The output will be as follows:

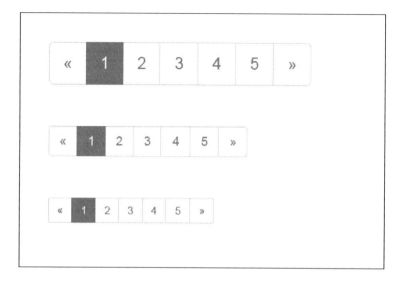

In the preceding output, you can see pagination being implemented. Let's see how it works. We used the .pagination class and implemented different sizes for each pagination, that is, pagination-lg (for larger sizes), pagination (for normal sizes), and pagination-sm (for smaller sizes).

We also used the .disabled class for the first box to denote that it is inactive and there are no pages to go left. Also, we used the .active class to depict the current page. Thus, this feature is awesome for forums and blog posts as well as to divide search results into several web pages for your custom search engine.

To depict the previous page and the next page to keep it simple, we use the .pager class.

Look at the following code snippet to understand this better:

```
<body  id="packt">
<h3><u><strong> Pager styles in Bootstrap </strong></u></h3>
<div>
    <ul class="pager">
        <li class="previous disabled"><a href="#">&larr; Previous</
a></li>
        <li class="next"><a href="#">Next &rarr;</a></li>
    </ul>
</div>
</body>
</html>
```

The output of this code will be as follows:

As you can see, it is quite simple to navigate through the webpage and this feature is very useful if the number of pages is limited and needs to be quickly surfed through.

List groups

The `list-group` component is used to display complex lists with custom content. You can add badges to lists in addition to using anchor tags instead of list elements. You can also use contextual colors to the lists.

Take a look at the following code so that you can understand this better:

```
<body id="packtpub">
<div>
    <div class="list-group">
        <a href="#" class="list-group-item active">
            <span class="glyphicon glyphicon-log-in"></span> Login
        </a>
        <a href="#" class="list-group-item">
            <span class="glyphicon glyphicon-facetime-video"></span>
Videos
        </a>
        <a href="#" class="list-group-item">
            <span class="glyphicon glyphicon-phone"></span> Customer
Care
        </a>
        <a href="#" class="list-group-item">
            <span class="glyphicon glyphicon-envelope"></span> Mail
        </a>
        <a href="#" class="list-group-item">
            <span class="glyphicon glyphicon-trash"></span> Trash
        </a>
        <a href="#" class="list-group-item">
            <span class="glyphicon glyphicon-off"></span> Logout
        </a>
    </div>
</div>
</body>
```

The output will be as follows:

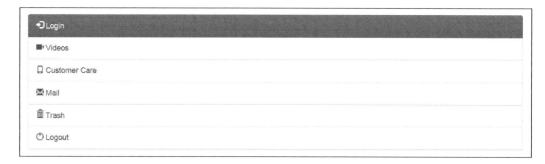

Thus, from the executed code you can see that the list group component helps us use anchor tags and can be used along with Glyphicons to improve the aesthetics. In the preceding code, we used the `.list-group` class to define the group and we listed the menu by assigning `.list-group-item` to each item in the group. The **Login** item is highlighted in blue since we defined the `.active` class along with it.

Button groups

Button groups are used to combine groups of buttons into a singular line. Using the `<div>` element, you need to wrap the buttons in a single group using the `.btn-group` class. We can also allocate the contextual colors to the buttons by adding the appropriate attribute.

Look at the following code to understand this better:

```
<body>
<div id="packt">
    <div class="btn-group">
        <button type="button" class="btn btn-info"> Inbox </button>
        <button type="button" class="btn btn-danger"> Spam </button>
        <button type="button" class="btn btn-success"> New Message </
button>
    </div>
</div>
</body>
```

The output of this code will be as follows:

As you can see, all the buttons are in the same line next to each other. The color of the buttons depends on the contextual color attribute assigned to it.

If you want to vertically stack the buttons instead of a horizontal display, then you need to use the `.btn-group-vertical` class.

Take a look at the following code snippet so that you can understand it better:

```
<body>
<div id="packt">
    <div class="btn-group-vertical">
        <button type="button" class="btn btn-info"> Inbox </button>
        <button type="button" class="btn btn-warning"> Spam </button>
        <button type="button" class="btn btn-success"> New Message </
button>
    </div>
</div>
</body>
```

The output will be as follows:

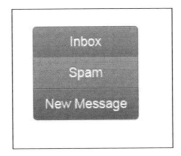

Let's assume that you need buttons of different sizes. You can get it by assigning button sizing classes to each button group instead of assigning the styles for each button.

Look at the code example to understand how it all works:

```
<body  id= "packt">
<div>
    <div class="btn-toolbar">
        <div class="btn-group btn-group-lg">
            <button type="button" class="btn btn-success"> Uno </button>
            <button type="button" class="btn btn-success"> Dos </button>
            <button type="button" class="btn btn-success"> Tres </button>
        </div>
    </div>
```

```
<br>
<div class="btn-toolbar">
    <div class="btn-group">
        <button type="button" class="btn btn-success"> Uno </button>
        <button type="button" class="btn btn-success"> Dos </button>
        <button type="button" class="btn btn-success"> Tres </button>
    </div>
</div>
<br>
<div class="btn-toolbar">
    <div class="btn-group btn-group-sm">
        <button type="button" class="btn btn-success"> Uno </button>
        <button type="button" class="btn btn-success"> Dos </button>
        <button type="button" class="btn btn-success"> Tres </button>
    </div>
</div>
<br>
<div class="btn-toolbar">
    <div class="btn-group btn-group-xs">
        <button type="button" class="btn btn-success"> Uno </button>
        <button type="button" class="btn btn-success"> Dos</button>
        <button type="button" class="btn btn-success"> Tres   </
button>
    </div>
</div>
</div>
</body>
```

The output of the code will be as follows:

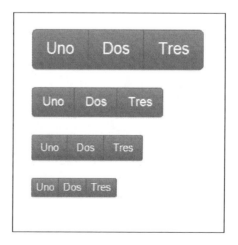

By adding the `.btn-group-lg`, `.btn-group-sm`, and `.btn-group-xs` classes to the `.btn-group` class, you can see that the output has buttons of a specific group in different sizes.

The button toolbar

If you want to group all the button groups together to create intricate components, you need to use the `.btn-toolbar` class.

Look at the following code to understand it better:

```
<body id="packt">
<div>
    <div class="btn-toolbar">
        <div class="btn-group">
            <button type="button" class="btn btn-info"> Alpha </button>
            <button type="button" class="btn btn-info"> Beta </button>
            <button type="button" class="btn btn-info"> Gamma </button>

        </div>
        <div class="btn-group">
           <button type="button" class="btn btn-success"> Uno </button>
           <button type="button" class="btn btn-success"> Dos </button>
           <button type="button" class="btn btn-success"> Tres </button>
        </div>
        <div class="btn-group">
           <button type="button" class="btn btn-danger"> One </button>
           <button type="button" class="btn btn-danger"> Two </button>
           <button type="button" class="btn btn-danger"> Three </button>
        </div>
    </div>
</div>
</body>
```

The output of this code will be as follows:

Therefore, you can see that the button groups have been combined using the button toolbar class.

Split button dropdowns

You can create a button drop-down menu in Bootstrap similar to the way you created drop-downs in the previous chapter. In this section, you will learn to create a split button drop-down.

Take a look at the following code to understand it better:

```
<body class="packt">
<div class="btn-group">
        <button class="btn btn-primary">Packt</button>
        <button data-toggle="dropdown" class="btn btn-primary
dropdown-toggle"><span class="caret"></span></button>
        <ul class="dropdown-menu">
            <li><a href="#"> Books and Videos </a></li>
            <li><a href="#"> Tech Hub </a></li>
            <li><a href="#"> Blog </a></li>
            <li class="divider"></li>
            <li><a href="#"> News Center </a></li>
            <li><a href="#"> Contact us </a></li>
            <li><a href="#"> Support </a></li>
        </ul>
    </div>
</body>
```

On execution, the output of this code will be a **Packt** button with a caret for the drop-down.

On clicking on the caret, the following drop-down menu will be displayed:

In the preceding code, we've created a **Packt** button and assigned the `dropdown` attribute to the `data-toggle` property. Then, we assigned the `.btn-primary` and `.dropdown-toggle` classes to it. Next, we created a caret and then defined a drop-down list of items using the `.dropdown-menu` class for the drop-down menu.

Justifying button groups

We use the `.btn-group-justified` class alongside the `.btn-group` class so that the button group spans the entire width of the parent element.

Take a look at the following code snippet to understand it better:

```
<body class="packt">
<div>
    <div class="btn-group btn-group-justified">
        <a href="#" class="btn btn-success"> Uno </a>
        <a href="#" class="btn btn-success"> Dos </a>
        <a href="#" class="btn btn-success"> Tres </a>
    </div>
</div>
</body>
```

The output of this code will be as follows:

Thus, the button group takes the entire block with a width of the parent element containing it.

Checkbox and radio buttons

Checkbox-styled and radio-styled buttons can be created in Bootstrap with relative ease and with different styles. You can select several checkbox buttons, but you cannot select more than one radio button.

Take a look at the following code so that you can understand the concepts of the checkbox button better:

```
<body>
<div id="packt">
    <div class="btn-group" data-toggle="buttons">
        <label class="btn btn-default">
```

```
                <input type="checkbox"> Inbox
        </label>
        <label class="btn btn-default">
                <input type="checkbox"> Spam
        </label>
        <label class="btn btn-default active">
                <input type="checkbox"> Compose
        </label>
    </div>
</div>
</body>
```

The output of this code will be as follows:

If you check the preceding code and the output, the `data-toggle="buttons"` property helps you to enable a checkbox kind of styling to the buttons in the group. You can also see that the `Compose` button is pre-checked as the `.active` class alongside the `.btn-default` class.

If you click on the **Inbox** and the **Spam** buttons, you will see that all three buttons get selected like checkboxes, where you can check multiple values.

Take a look at the following code to understand the procedure of enabling radio-styled functionality to buttons:

```
<body>
<div id="packt">
    <div class="btn-group" data-toggle="buttons">
        <label class="btn btn-default">
          <input type="radio" name="options" id="option1"> Radio 1
        </label>
        <label class="btn btn-default">
          <input type="radio" name="options" id="option2"> Radio 2
        </label>
        <label class="btn btn-default  active">
          <input type="radio" name="options" id="option3"> Radio 3
        </label>
    </div>
</div>
</body>
```

The output of this code will be as follows:

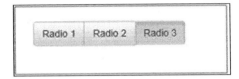

If you observe the preceding output, the **Radio 3** button is highlighted due to the `.active` class assigned to it. However, unlike the checkbox functionality, you can select only a single radio button at a given time, thereby displaying radio-style functionality.

Alerts

Alerts are used to convey crucial messages for situations where the website users have to be warned, informed, or cautioned, that results in immediate attention from them.

Look at the following code to understand this better:

```
<body id="packt">
<div>
    <div class="alert alert-info">
        <a href="#" class="close" data-dismiss="alert">&times;</a>
        <em>Information: </em> <u>Bootstrap is an amazing utility</u>
    </div>
    <div class="alert alert-danger">
        <a href="#" class="close" data-dismiss="alert">&times;</a>
        <em>Warning! </em> <u>Malware found</u>
    </div>
     <div class="alert alert-warning">
        <a href="#" class="close" data-dismiss="alert">&times;</a>
        <em>Proceed with Caution: </em><u> Website may have viruses
and spyware</u>
    </div>
     <div class="alert alert-success">
        <a href="#" class="close" data-dismiss="alert">&times;</a>
        <em>Wow: </em> <u>You won</u>
    </div>
</div>
</body>
```

The output will be as follows:

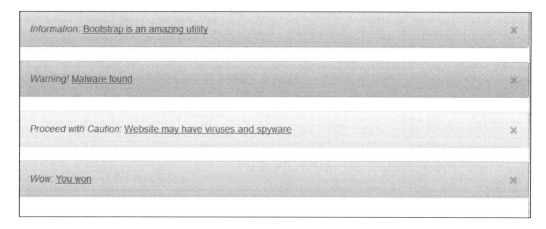

As you can see, the alert messages are contextually used according to the relevant scenario.

In the preceding code, you can see that we used the `.alert-info`, `.alert-danger`, `.alert-warning`, and `.alert-success` classes to convey certain messages. We also defined the `data-dismiss="alert"` attribute in conjunction with the `.close` class, which will enable your website users to dismiss the alert. Once you click on the close symbol, the alert will be dismissed owing to the functionality of the Bootstrap JavaScript library.

You can also use the `.alert-link` class to provide contextual color links with an alert.

Take a look at the following code so that you can understand it better:

```
<body id="packt">
  <div class="alert alert-success">

  <a href="#" class="alert-link"> Eureka, Click for the next stage </
a>

  </div>

  <div class="alert alert-info">

  <a href="#" class="alert-link">Welcome to the Next stage</a>

  </div>
```

```
<div class="alert alert-warning">

<a href="#" class="alert-link"> Caution! You will lose the game </a>

    </div>

<div class="alert alert-danger">

<a href="#" class="alert-link"> Click here to eradicate malware </a>

</div>

</body>
```

The output of this code will be as follows:

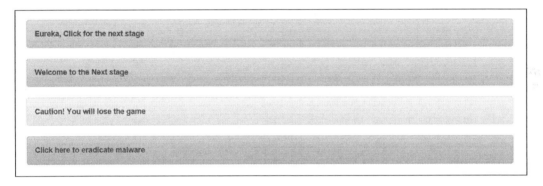

In the preceding code, we created alert links for the web page, which can either redirect the user or take a further step.

Media objects

You can abstract object styles for building components such as blog posts using media objects, wherein the media is aligned alongside textual content. The media can be used inside a list too, which is a handy feature for comments and forums.

Look at the following code to understand this better:

```
<body id="packt">
 <ul class="media-list">
  <li class="media">
    <a class="pull-left" href="#">
      <video  class="media-object" width="150" height="100" id=
"packt" controls= "controls" autoplay="autoplay">
```

```
      <source src ="http://clips.vorwaerts-gmbh.de/big_buck_bunny.mp4" />
    </video>
        </a>
        <div class="media-body">
          <h4 class="media-heading">Sample video</h4>
          The following is a video sample to demonstrate the media object
    feature
        </div>
      </li>
    </ul>
  </body>
```

The output of this code will be as follows:

Sample video

The following is a video sample to demonstrate the media object feature

In the preceding code, we used the `.media-list` class in which we added the `.media` class. In this example, we used a video but you can use other media types such as images too. Then we defined the `.media-object` class and later on we added the relevant textual content inside the `.media-body` class.

Responsive scalable embed

The responsive embed feature allows browsers to determine video dimensions based on the block they are embedded into by means of a ratio, which helps in scalability depending on the screen size of various devices.

Look at the following code to understand this better:

```
<!DOCTYPE html>
<html>
<head>
<meta name="viewport" content="width=device-width, initial-scale=1">
<title> Responsive video embed feature </title>
<link rel="stylesheet" href="http://maxcdn.bootstrapcdn.com/
bootstrap/3.2.0/css/bootstrap.min.css">
<link rel="stylesheet" href="http://maxcdn.bootstrapcdn.com/
bootstrap/3.2.0/css/bootstrap-theme.min.css">
```

```
<script src="http://ajax.googleapis.com/ajax/libs/jquery/1.11.1/
jquery.min.js"></script>
<script src="http://maxcdn.bootstrapcdn.com/bootstrap/3.2.0/js/
bootstrap.min.js"></script>
<style type="text/css">
       #packtpub{
         margin-left: 25px;
          margin-top: 30px;
                   }
</style>
</head>
<body id="packtpub">
<div class="container">
 <div class="panel panel-info">
  <div class="panel-heading">
  <p class="panel-title"> Video Embedded in a panel </p>
   <div class="panel-body">
     <div class="embed-responsive embed-responsive-16by9 hidden-xs">
      <iframe class="embed-responsive-item" src="http://clips.
vorwaerts-gmbh.de/big_buck_bunny.mp4"></iframe>
     </div>
    </div>
   </div>
  </div>
</div>
</body>
</html>
```

The output will be as follows:

Let's go through the code to see how it all works. First, we created a panel in which we will embed a video. Then, we defined the panel title, panel heading, and the panel body.

Then, we use the following code to help us embed the video in the panel:

```
<div class="embed-responsive embed-responsive-16by9 hidden-xs">
    <iframe class="embed-responsive-item" src="http://clips.
vorwaerts-gmbh.de/big_buck_bunny.mp4"></iframe>
    </div>
```

In the highlighted code, we used the 16by9 ratio with the .embed-responsive-16by9 class. Then, we've included the .hidden-xs class, which ensures that though the video is responsive and scales according to the device used, the video will be hidden in the extra small device. Within the <iframe> element, we include the .embed-responsive-item class and the source of the video.

If you decrease the screen size by minimizing the width and height of your browser or use a small screen device such as a smart phone or a tablet, then you will observe that the video is responsive and scales accordingly. However, when you decrease the screen size to the *extra-small* level, the video is hidden and not visible to the users.

In the following screenshot, it is quite obvious that the video is hidden when you decrease the screen size to the xs (extra-small) level:

Video Embedded in a panel

Summary

In this chapter, we had a look at the widely-used components of Bootstrap that help you design your webpage with relative ease. The simplification of the evolution process of a website, from post-mockup skeleton to fully-fledged web application, has increased significantly over time, mainly due to a modular approach. You can extend or customize the components, and this code reusability is the paradigm of the DRY principle. In the next chapter, we'll take a look at enhancing your Bootstrap experience with JavaScript.

7
Enhancing User Experience with JavaScript

In the previous chapter, we had a look at the various components in Bootstrap. Bootstrap comes with official baked-in jQuery plugins, which helps you to build a dynamic website. You can develop a creative website by just including the plugins and further customizing it with JavaScript as well as data attributes. In this chapter, we'll take a look at enriching the user experience with JavaScript and jQuery plugins. There are many ways to use the plugins, but we'll show you easier ways to incorporate it to help you get to grips with them.

We'll be covering the following popular plugins in this chapter:

- Tooltip
- Popovers
- ScrollSpy
- Collapse with Accordion
- Modals
- Carousel

Streamlining your projects with official plugins

Since most of the plugins have a dependency on jQuery, you have to include the CDN link for jQuery or include the jQuery file in your code by downloading the file from the official website. In this chapter, we're using the CDN link for all the examples including the Bootstrap JavaScript and theme file.

The `<head>` section for all the coding examples will include the following links:

```
<link rel="stylesheet" href="http://maxcdn.bootstrapcdn.com/
bootstrap/3.2.0/css/bootstrap.min.css">
<link rel="stylesheet" href="http://maxcdn.bootstrapcdn.com/
bootstrap/3.2.0/css/bootstrap-theme.min.css">
<script src="http://ajax.googleapis.com/ajax/libs/jquery/1.11.1/
jquery.min.js"></script>
<script  src="http://maxcdn.bootstrapcdn.com/bootstrap/3.2.0/js/
bootstrap.min.js"></script>
```

Now, let's take a look at the popular plugins, which you can incorporate in your code to build aesthetic websites.

Tooltips

Tooltips are used to depict information or hint for icons, links, and buttons whenever you hover your mouse over them. As soon as you hover your mouse over the element, it displays the relevant information as defined in the code, thereby assisting your website users to know the purpose of those items or links.

Take a look at the following code example to understand this better:

```
<!DOCTYPE html>
<html>
<head>
<title>Bootstrap ToolTips with Placement using JavaScript</title>
<link rel="stylesheet" href="http://maxcdn.bootstrapcdn.com/
bootstrap/3.2.0/css/bootstrap.min.css">
<link rel="stylesheet" href="http://maxcdn.bootstrapcdn.com/
bootstrap/3.2.0/css/bootstrap-theme.min.css">
<script src="http://ajax.googleapis.com/ajax/libs/jquery/1.11.1/
jquery.min.js"></script>
<script src="http://maxcdn.bootstrapcdn.com/bootstrap/3.2.0/js/
bootstrap.min.js"></script>
<script type="text/javascript">
$(document).ready(function(){
    $(".packtpub1").tooltip({
        placement : 'left'
    });
    $(".packtpub2").tooltip({
        placement : 'top'
    });
    $(".packtpub3").tooltip({
        placement : 'right'
    });
    $(".packtpub4").tooltip({
        placement : 'bottom'
```

```
        });
    });
    </script>
    <style type="text/css">
      #packt{
          padding: 150px 150px 150px 150px;
                    }
    </style>
    </head>
    <body id="packt">
    <div>
    <button type="button" class="btn btn-primary packtpub1" data-
    toggle="tooltip"  title="Left Tooltip"> Hey Joe </button>
    <hr><br><br>
    <button type="button" class="btn btn-primary packtpub2" data-
    toggle="tooltip"  title="Top Tooltip"> Hey Joe </button>
    <hr><br><br>
    <button type="button" class="btn btn-primary packtpub3" data-
    toggle="tooltip"  title="Right ToolTip"> Hey Joe </button>
    <hr><br><br>
    <button type="button" class="btn btn-primary packtpub4" data-
    toggle="tooltip"  title="Bottom ToolTip"> Hey Joe </button>
    </div>
    </body>
    </html>
```

The output of this code will be as follows:

In this example, let's hover over the second button, where the tooltip is defined to be on top of the button. The output upon hovering will be as follows:

As you can see, the tooltip for the second button is on the top of the element and has been defined as **Top Tooltip** in the title of the second button. In the preceding code, we defined the placement in the JavaScript code, resulting in tooltips being displayed on the left of the first button, top of the second button, right of the third button, and bottom of the fourth button. We used the `data-toggle` attribute, to which we have assigned the `tooltip` value.

Popovers

Popovers are used for housing secondary information for any element by adding small overlays of content. It is particularly useful as you can display elements such as links and image tags, including other `<div>` elements.

Take a look at the following code to help you understand it better:

```
<!DOCTYPE html>
<html>
<head>
<title>Bootstrap Popovers</title>
```

```
<link rel="stylesheet" href="http://maxcdn.bootstrapcdn.com/
bootstrap/3.2.0/css/bootstrap.min.css">
<link rel="stylesheet" href="http://maxcdn.bootstrapcdn.com/
bootstrap/3.2.0/css/bootstrap-theme.min.css">
<script src="http://ajax.googleapis.com/ajax/libs/jquery/1.11.1/
jquery.min.js"></script>
<script src="http://maxcdn.bootstrapcdn.com/bootstrap/3.2.0/js/
bootstrap.min.js"></script>
<script type="text/javascript">
$(document).ready(function(){
    $(".packtpub a").popover({
        placement : 'top'
    });
});
$(document).ready(function(){
    $(".pubman a").popover({
        placement : 'bottom'
    });
});
</script>
<style type="text/css">
  #packt{
      padding: 150px 175px 175px 175px;
      }
</style>
</head>
<body id="packt">
<div>
    <ul class="packtpub">
        <li><a href="#" class="btn btn-default" data-toggle="popover"
title="Musician" data-content="Awesome Vocalist">Jim Morrison</a></li>
        <hr><br>
        <li><a href="#" class="btn btn-success" data-toggle="popover"
title="Scientist" data-content="Awesome Thinker">Stephen Hawking</a></
li>
        <hr><br>
    </ul>
 </div>
 <div>
        <ul class="pubman">
    <li><a href="#" class="btn btn-danger" data-toggle="popover"
title="Musician" data-content="Amazing guitarist">Jimi Hendrix</a></
li>
        <hr><br>
        <li><a href="#" class="btn btn-primary" data-toggle="popover"
title="Philosopher" data-content="Rational Thinker">Socrates</a></li>
    </ul>
</div>
</body>
</html>
```

The output will be as follows:

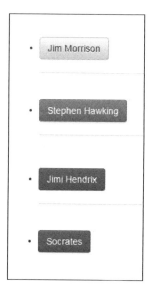

Let's now click on the first button (**Jim Morrison**) and the fourth button (**Socrates**). On clicking, we will get the following output:

As you can see, **Jim Morrison** is defined in the `title` attribute of the code as **Musician** and **Awesome Vocalist** as the content defined by the `data-content` attribute. Similarly, by clicking on **Socrates** you can see **Philosopher** as defined in the `title` attribute of the code and the content defined as **Rational Thinker** in the `data-content` attribute. In the preceding code, we defined one list using the `.packtpub` class and the other using the `.pubman` class. The `data-toggle` attribute specifies the element which controls the popover. The `data-content` attribute specifies the content depicted inside the popover, and the placement defines the position of the popover. In the output, if you click on all the buttons with the `.packtpub` class, you can see the placement of the popover is on top, whereas the buttons with the `.pubman` class have their popover placed on the bottom of the buttons.

Accordion

To manage comprehensive content, we use the `.collapse` class with accordion, using which we can expand or stretch to reveal the content associated with that item. This feature is quite handy and can be used in conjunction with panels to subtly depict a large amount of content.

Take a look at the following code to understand it better:

```html
<!DOCTYPE html>
<html>
<head>
<title>Collapse Functionality with Accordion</title>
<link rel="stylesheet" href="http://maxcdn.bootstrapcdn.com/
bootstrap/3.2.0/css/bootstrap.min.css">
<link rel="stylesheet" href="http://maxcdn.bootstrapcdn.com/
bootstrap/3.2.0/css/bootstrap-theme.min.css">
<script src="http://ajax.googleapis.com/ajax/libs/jquery/1.11.1/
jquery.min.js"></script>
<script src="http://maxcdn.bootstrapcdn.com/bootstrap/3.2.0/js/
bootstrap.min.js"></script>
<style type="text/css">
    #packt{
        padding: 35px 35px 35px 35px;
    }
</style>
</head>
<body id="packt">
    <div class="panel-group" id="accordion">
        <div class="panel panel-success">
            <div class="panel-heading">
                <h4 class="panel-title">
```

```
                                    <a data-toggle="collapse" data-parent="#accordion"
           href="#packtpubcollapse1">WebRTC</a>
                          </h4>
                    </div>
                    <div id="packtpubcollapse1" class="panel-collapse collapse
           in">
                          <div class="panel-body">
                <p>WebRTC(Web Real-Time Communication) enables web developers
           to write real-time multimedia applications for theWeb which can be
           deployed across multiple platforms, without the need for intermediate
           software or plugins.WebRTC enables Peer-to-Peer, browser-to-
           browser communication and is widely used for web-based phone
           calling, conferencing, enterprise contact centres, and educational
           apps. The resourceful and interactive nature of WebRTC makes it an
           excellent utilityofchoice for real-time web application development.
           <a href="https://www.packtpub.com/books/content/webrtc"> More
           information</a></p>
                              </div>
                          </div>
                    </div>
                <div class="panel panel-primary">
                          <div class="panel-heading">
                              <h4 class="panel-title">
                                    <a data-toggle="collapse" data-parent="#accordion"
           href="#packtpubcollapse2">Meteor</a>
                              </h4>
                          </div>
                          <div id="packtpubcollapse2" class="panel-collapse
           collapse">
                              <div class="panel-body">
                                    <p>Meteor is an open-source web application
           framework which follows the MVVM pattern.Meteor runs on both the
           server-side as well as the client-side, since both share the
           same database API. Meteor is written in pure JavaScript and uses
           established design patterns, easing the pain of the tedious tasks of
           web application development, helping you build robust applications in
           very little time. <a href="https://www.packtpub.com/books/content/
           meteor-meteor-js">More information</a></p>
                              </div>
                          </div>
                    </div>
                </div>
           </body>
           </html>
```

The output of this code will be as follows:

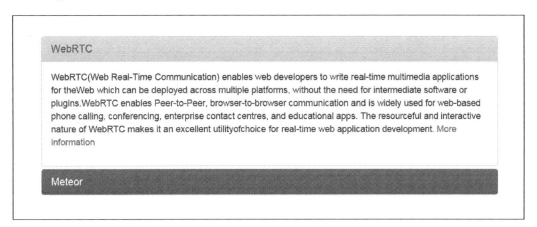

If you click on **Meteor** in the panel below **WebRTC** in the output, you can see that the **WebRTC** panel collapses and the **Meteor** panel is displayed. Therefore, the output will be as displayed as in the following screenshot:

As you can see, the accordion feature is quite useful to manage large amounts of content. In the preceding code, we defined the data attributes by assigning the value `accordion` as `data-parent` in addition to defining `collapse` as the value for the `data-toggle` attribute. We have defined the panels and used the `.panel-collapse` class in conjunction with the `.collapse` and `.collapse in` classes. While `collapse` hides the content, the `.collapse in` class shows the content. Therefore, we have defined the first panel with the `.collapse in` class so that the first panel is active and displays information by default.

ScrollSpy

If you have a web page with a lot of content that runs to more than a single page, **ScrollSpy** is the solution for such navigation. It is especially used in conjunction with the navbar. The navigation menu gets highlighted based on the scroll position, thereby providing high accessibility to your website users.

Since the code is too large to fit in to a single page, we will discuss it part by part. You can always refer to the code bundle to see the entire code at once.

In the `<head>` section, we include all the relevant links and define the scroll-area:

```
<!DOCTYPE html>
<html>
<head>
<title>Scrollspy in Bootstrap</title>
<link rel="stylesheet" href="http://maxcdn.bootstrapcdn.com/
bootstrap/3.2.0/css/bootstrap.min.css">
<link rel="stylesheet" href="http://maxcdn.bootstrapcdn.com/
bootstrap/3.2.0/css/bootstrap-theme.min.css">
<script src="http://ajax.googleapis.com/ajax/libs/jquery/1.11.1/
jquery.min.js"></script>
<script src="http://maxcdn.bootstrapcdn.com/bootstrap/3.2.0/js/
bootstrap.min.js"></script>
<style type="text/css">
.scroll-area {
  height: 500px;
  position: relative;
  overflow: auto;
}
#packt
    {padding: 30px 30px 30px 30px;}
    </style>
</head>
```

Then, we create a parent `<div>` element with the `.container` class in which we will put all our code, and then at the end of the following code samples, which will be incorporated in the complete code, we will close the `.container` class' `</div>` element.

After, we create a navbar and also include a drop-down menu in one of the navbar list items:

```
<h2>ScrollSpy</h2>
    <p>The ScrollSpy plugin is quite useful for automatically updating
nav targets based on scroll position. When you scroll the area below
the navbar,you can witness the change in the active class.It works for
dropdowns too.</p>
    <nav id="myNavbar" class="navbar navbar-default"
role="navigation">
        <!-- Brand and toggle get grouped for better mobile display
-->
        <div class="navbar-header">
            <button type="button" class="navbar-toggle" data-
toggle="collapse" data-target="#navbarCollapse">
                <span class="sr-only">Toggle navigation</span>
                <span class="icon-bar"></span>
                <span class="icon-bar"></span>
                <span class="icon-bar"></span>
            </button>
            <a class="navbar-brand" href="#">Packt Publishing </a>
        </div>
        <div class="collapse navbar-collapse" id="navbarCollapse">
            <ul class="nav navbar-nav">
                <li class="active"><a href="#packt1">Packt
Information</a></li>
                <li><a href="#packt2">Ordering information</a></li>
                <li><a href="#packt3">Terms and Conditions</a></li>
                <li class="dropdown"><a href="#" class="dropdown-
toggle" data-toggle="dropdown">Blogs and Primers<b class="caret"></
b></a>
                    <ul class="dropdown-menu">
                        <li><a href="#packtsub1">Blog</a></li>
                        <li><a href="#packtsub2">Tech Hub</a></li>
                        <li><a href="#packtsub3">Articles</a></li>
                    </ul>
                </li>

            </ul>
    </div>
        </nav>
```

Following that, we create a `div` class and assign it the `.scroll-area` class and use data attributes such as adding `data-spy="scroll"` to enable the ScrollSpy behavior in addition to using `data-target="#myNavbar"` to select the navbar.

In the following code, the content in the paragraph is huge, so we will just refer to it as some text. However, you can refer to the entire content of the paragraph from the code bundle.

The code will look like this:

```html
<div class="scroll-area" data-spy="scroll" data-target="#myNavbar"
data-offset="0">
        <h1 id="packt1"> Packt Info </h1>
        <p> ...Some text here... </p>

        <hr>
        <h1 id="packt2"> How Pre-Orders Work </h1>
        <p> ... Some text here... </p>
        <hr>
        <h1 id="packt3"> Packt's Terms and Conditions</h1>
        <p> ...Some text here... </p>
        <hr>
        <h1>Blogs and Primers: One stop Technical Hub </h1>
        <p> ... Some text here... </p>
        <h2 id="packtsub1">Golang Blog</h2>
        <p> ...Some text here... </p>

        <h2 id="packtsub2">Technical Hub for PhpStorm</h4>
        <p> ...Some text here... </p>
        <h2 id="packtsub3">Article about Foundation</h2>
        <p> ...Some text here... </p>
        <hr>
        </div>
```

If you want to refer to the entire code, you need to refer to the ScrollSpy code in the code bundle. The output of the code will be as follows:

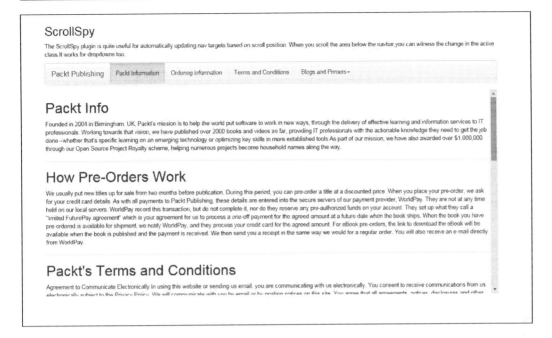

When you click on any item in the navbar, you will go to the respective paragraph as defined in the code; for example, if you choose any options in the drop-down menu under **Blogs and Primers**, it will scroll to that specific paragraph thereby enabling effective accessibility to your website users.

If you scroll down to **Packt's Terms and Conditions**, you can see the following screen:

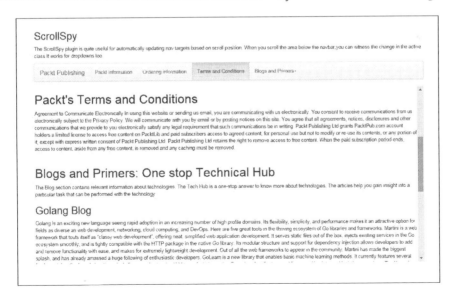

You can observe that when you scroll down to **Packt's Terms and Conditions**, the **Terms and Conditions** item in the navigation bar gets highlighted. Thus, when you scroll to a specific paragraph, it will highlight the respective item that defines it.

Modals

A modal is a type of a dialog box that provides crucial information to your website users or educates the users prior to taking any decisive action on the website. A modal can be a confirmation, a warning, an informative dialog, or a dialog with a form that asks for some information from the user or something mundane, such as a login dialog for session timeout; for example, you are about to erase important data or click on a malicious link. The modal provides information that will help you decide whether you want to take a step forward in relation to an action.

Take a look at the following code so that you understand it better:

```html
<!DOCTYPE html>
<html>
<head>
<title> Bootstrap 3 Modals </title>
<link rel="stylesheet" href="http://maxcdn.bootstrapcdn.com/
bootstrap/3.2.0/css/bootstrap.min.css">
<link rel="stylesheet" href="http://maxcdn.bootstrapcdn.com/
bootstrap/3.2.0/css/bootstrap-theme.min.css">
<script src="http://ajax.googleapis.com/ajax/libs/jquery/1.11.1/
jquery.min.js"></script>
<script src="http://maxcdn.bootstrapcdn.com/bootstrap/3.2.0/js/
bootstrap.min.js"></script>
<script type="text/javascript">
  $(document).ready(function(){
    $("#packtpub").modal('show');
  });
</script>
  <style>
      #packt { padding: 30px 30px 30px 30px; }
  </style>
</head>
<body id="packt">
<div id="packtpub" class="modal fade">
    <div class="modal-dialog">
        <div class="modal-content">
            <div class="modal-header">
                <button type="button" class="close" data-
dismiss="modal" aria-hidden="true">&times;</button>
                <h1 class="modal-title">Beware</h1>
```

```
            </div>
            <div class="modal-body">
                <p>The Site has been blocked due to malicious
content</p>
                <p class="text-warning"><small> Proceed at your own
risk</small></p>
            </div>
            <div class="modal-footer">
                <button type="button" class="btn btn-primary" data-
dismiss="modal">Quit</button>
                <button type="button" class="btn btn-danger">Proceed</
button>
            </div>
        </div>
    </div>
</div>
</body>
</html>
```

The output of this code will be as follows:

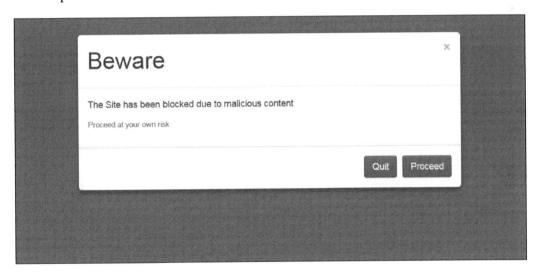

As you can see from the preceding output, we created a modal that warns the user if they are about to access a malicious website or click on a malicious link.

From the preceding code, you can see that we used the `.modal-dialog` class, which will create a dialog box and the `.modal-content` class that will define the content in the dialog box. After that, we defined `modal-header`, `modal-body`, and `modal-footer`, where we have put the relevant content. We have also used contextual colors for the buttons to make it look genuine and apt for the purpose.

Carousels

A carousel is a presentation of content in a cyclic manner wherein the text and images are made visible or accessible in a slideshow format. In the following code example, we will use data attributes such as `data-slide`, `data-interval`, and `data-ride` to create the carousel functionality. The `data-ride="carousel"` attribute is used to mark a carousel as animation starting at page load. The `data-slide` attribute changes the position of the slide to the current position and is used to navigate to previous and next items. The `data-slide-to` attribute is used for a slide index for the carousel slides, thereby helping you create web pages consisting of image galleries. The `data-interval` attribute decides the time delay between the cycling of slides.

Take a look at the following code to understand this better:

```
<!DOCTYPE html>
<html>
<head>
<title> Bootstrap 3 Carousels </title>
<link rel="stylesheet" href="http://maxcdn.bootstrapcdn.com/
bootstrap/3.2.0/css/bootstrap.min.css">
<link rel="stylesheet" href="http://maxcdn.bootstrapcdn.com/
bootstrap/3.2.0/css/bootstrap-theme.min.css">
<script src="http://ajax.googleapis.com/ajax/libs/jquery/1.11.1/
jquery.min.js"></script>
<script src="http://maxcdn.bootstrapcdn.com/bootstrap/3.2.0/js/
bootstrap.min.js"></script>
<style type="text/css">

.item{
    background: #333;
    text-align: center;
    height: 300px !important;
}
.carousel{
    margin-top: 20px;
}
.packt{
  padding: 30px 30px 30px 30px;
}
</style>
</head>
<body class="packt">
```

```
    <div id="myCarousel" class="carousel slide" data-interval="500"
data-ride="carousel">
      <!-- Carousel indicators -->
        <ol class="carousel-indicators">
           <li data-target="#myCarousel" data-slide-to="0"
class="active"></li>
           <li data-target="#myCarousel" data-slide-to="1"></li>
           <li data-target="#myCarousel" data-slide-to="2"></li>
        </ol>
      <!-- Carousel items -->
        <div class="carousel-inner">
           <div class="active item">
              <img src="Packt1.png" alt="Packt">
              <div class="carousel-caption">
                <h6><b>Packt: Always finding a way </b></h6>
                </div>
           </div>
           <div class="item">
    <img src="Packt2.png" alt="PacktLib">
                <div class="carousel-caption">
                <h6><b>Packt: Always finding a way </b></h6>
              </div>
           </div>
           <div class="item">
    <img src="Packt3.png" alt="Packt">
                <div class="carousel-caption">
                 <h6><b>Packt: Always finding a way </b></h6>
                </div>
           </div>
        </div>
        <!-- Carousel nav -->
        <a class="carousel-control left" href="#myCarousel" data-
slide="prev">
            <span class="glyphicon glyphicon-chevron-left"></span>
        </a>
        <a class="carousel-control right" href="#myCarousel" data-
slide="next">
            <span class="glyphicon glyphicon-chevron-right"></span>
        </a>
    </div>
</body>
</html>
```

The output of this code will display an image gallery with a carousel caption (**Packt: Always finding a way**) as defined in the code:

By the use of Glyphicons, we also defined the symbols for the `prev` and `next` functionalities. Also, for the first image, we used the `.active` class alongside the `.item` class to set it as the first default slide that your website user will see on executing the preceding code.

Summary

In this chapter, we took a look at the widely-used official jQuery plugins that help you to create modals, carousels, and other complex facets in a jiffy. In the next chapter, you will learn about several Bootstrap utilities including third-party plugins and resources which you can use to streamline your web designing process with Bootstrap.

8
Bootstrap Technical Hub – A One-stop Shop for Powerful Bootstrap Utilities

Web designing has a steep learning curve, especially when you are in the process of building intricate websites with complex functionality. In the past, you would be engrossed in developing the entire functionality with the aid of JavaScript. However, with the advent of batteries-loaded frameworks such as Bootstrap, the development process has become easier, thereby lowering the learning curve significantly.

Bootstrap has gained immense popularity and there are several ready-made themes, templates, snippets, plugins, and editors that simplify the art of website creation. Some of the toolkits help you streamline your development process to such an extent that you can create a website in a matter of minutes. Apart from the official plugins and components, there are hundreds of resources built around Bootstrap that can help you get to grips with powerful web designing.

In this chapter, you'll learn the imperative utilities in brief so that you will be able to use them for your projects. We'll section the utilities according to their categories, which are as follows:

- Themes and templates
- Ready-made resources and plugins
- Development tools and editors

- Official Bootstrap resources
  - ◦ Bootlint
  - ◦ Bootstrap for SaaS
  - ◦ Bootstrap Expo

Now that we've defined what you'll be learning, let's take a look at each category.

Themes and templates

We'll now look at some of the free as well as commercial tailored themes and templates that help you build websites quickly and accurately, saving you significant time and effort and freeing you to focus on more important things in your web development projects.

Open source themes and templates

There are many websites that offer themes and templates absolutely free in addition to them being used for personal as well as commercial use. The following are a few of them:

- **Start Bootstrap** (`http://startbootstrap.com/`): Start Bootstrap is an open source library of Bootstrap 3 themes and templates which are tailor-made for specific purposes such as an e-commerce website or an admin dashboard. You can use them for personal and commercial use.

- **Bootswatch** (`http://bootswatch.com/`): Bootswatch offers free themes that you can have by simply downloading the CSS file and replacing the one in Bootstrap. Bootswatch implements a modular approach where the changes are contained in just two LESS files resulting in easy maintenance, simple modification, and ensuring forward compatibility. It also has an API that helps you integrate those themes with your platform.

- **Black Tie** (`http://www.blacktie.co/`): Black Tie has a collection of modern themes that you can download and even customize as per your requirement. It is quite a useful source as some of the themes are tailored for conjunction with several platforms such as Tumblr, Drupal, and Wordpress.

- **Bootstrap Zero** (`http://bootstrapzero.com/`): Bootstrap Zero is one of the largest free template collections for the Bootstrap platform. It has accumulated the best and widely-used templates from various sources, and you can find just about any template here. The makers of Bootstrap Zero are working on including toolkits and other resources on their website to make it a one-stop destination for Bootstrap third-party add-ons.

- **Bootplus** (`http://aozora.github.io/bootplus/`): Bootplus is a sleek and intuitive Google-styled frontend framework to streamline web designing using Bootstrap.

- **Fbootstrapp** (`http://ckrack.github.io/fbootstrapp/`): Fbootstrapp is a toolkit that helps you kick start the development of Facebook-styled iframe apps.

- **Bootmetro** (`http://aozora.github.io/bootmetro/`): Bootmetro is a framework that helps you develop modern intuitive web apps with the look and feel of Windows 8, including compatibility with modern browsers such as Chrome, Firefox, and Opera.

Sites such as GetTemplate (`http://www.gettemplate.com/`), Flatstrap (`http://flatstrap.org/`), Cardeostrap (`http://cardeostrap.cardeo.ca/`), VegiThemes (`http://vegibit.com/vegithemes-twitter-bootstrap-themes/`), and Bootstrap Taste (`http://bootstraptaste.com/`) do have a sizeable count of themes and templates that will help you develop webpages in an hour's time.

Commercial themes and templates

Apart from the abundant free themes and templates, there are commercial ready-made themes and templates that come at an affordable price which you can implement for your business needs. The themes and templates are specifically created for those customers who want a quick-fix solution related to web design for their organization.

Following are the various websites that host a wide array of themes and templates:

- **Wrapbootstrap** (`https://wrapbootstrap.com/`)

- **Theme Forest** (`http://themeforest.net/`)

- **Design Modo** (`http://designmodo.com/shop/?u=787`)

- **Grid Gum** (`http://gridgum.com/themes/category/bootstrap-themes/`)

- **Bootstrap Bay** (`http://bootstrapbay.com/`)

- **Bootstrap Made** (`https://bootstrapmade.com/`)

- **Creative Market** (`https://creativemarket.com/themes/bootstrap`)

- **PixelKit** (`http://pixelkit.com/`)

Ready-made resources and plugins

There are several resources and toolkits to streamline Bootstrap web development. Let's take a look at the most widely-used and efficient ones that will help you develop your website faster and with great accuracy.

Font Awesome

The **Font Awesome** library is a collection of hundreds of icons that aid you in building web pages. The scalable vector icons can be customized by CSS in addition to providing high resolution displays. You can either download it or use the Bootstrap CDN at MaxCDN.

In the following example, we'll be using the CDN to understand how it all works:

```
<!DOCTYPE html>
<html>
  <head>
    <title>Font Awesome example</title>
    <meta name="viewport" content="width=device-width, initial-
scale=1.0">
    <link rel="stylesheet" href="https://maxcdn.bootstrapcdn.com/
bootstrap/3.2.0/css/bootstrap.min.css">
   <script src="https://maxcdn.bootstrapcdn.com/bootstrap/3.2.0/js/
bootstrap.min.js"></script>
 <link href="https://maxcdn.bootstrapcdn.com/font-awesome/4.2.0/css/
font-awesome.min.css" rel="stylesheet">
<style> #packt {padding :40px 40px 40px 40px}</style>
</head>
<body id="packt">
<i class="fa fa-camera-retro fa-lg"></i> fa-lg
<br><i class="fa fa-camera-retro fa-2x"></i> fa-2x
<br><i class="fa fa-camera-retro fa-3x"></i> fa-3x
<br><i class="fa fa-camera-retro fa-4x"></i> fa-4x
<br><i class="fa fa-camera-retro fa-5x"></i> fa-5x
</body>
</html>
```

The output of this code is as follows:

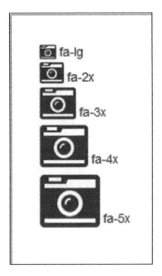

From the output, you can see that we used a camera retro icon. Now you can add the CSS prefix, `fa`, followed by the icon name. In the example, you can see the icon increasing in size owing to the `fa-lg`, `fa-2x`, `fa-3x`, `fa-4x`, and `fa-5x` class assigned to it.

You can download the Font Awesome icons from their official website `http://fontawesome.io/`.

Social Buttons for Bootstrap

The Social Buttons website `http://lipis.github.io/bootstrap-social/` has a collection of all icons related to social media. From Dropbox to Twitter, this includes everything that is prevalent. The dependencies are on Font Awesome and Bootstrap; therefore, you can use the same CDN links used in the Bootstrap and Font Awesome code in addition to incorporating `bootstrap-social.css` for CSS or `bootstrap-social.less` for LESS files to get started with it. More relevant information can be found on its official website.

Bootstrap Magic

Bootstrap Magic is a theme editor to create themes quickly. With attributes such as `typeahead`, `auto-complete`, and `instant live preview`, it helps you to build themes in addition to importing the modified LESS variables or saving the CSS and LESS files.

More information can be found on its official website at `http://pikock.github.io/bootstrap-magic/app/index.html#!/editor`.

Jasny Bootstrap

Jasny Bootstrap is a toolkit that provides additional features and components tailored to help you enhance your Bootstrap web designing projects. Basically, it is an extension to Bootstrap. You can either download the CSS and JavaScript files or use the following CDNs:

```
<link rel="stylesheet" href="//cdnjs.cloudflare.com/ajax/libs/jasny-
bootstrap/3.1.3/css/jasny-bootstrap.min.css">
<script src="//cdnjs.cloudflare.com/ajax/libs/jasny-bootstrap/3.1.3/
js/jasny-bootstrap.min.js"></script>
```

Take a look at the following simple code example where we add labels to the buttons, thereby enhancing the aesthetics of our web design:

```
<!DOCTYPE html>
<html>
<head>
<title> Jasny Bootstrap </title>
<link rel="stylesheet" href="http://maxcdn.bootstrapcdn.com/
bootstrap/3.2.0/css/bootstrap.min.css">
<link rel="stylesheet" href="http://maxcdn.bootstrapcdn.com/
bootstrap/3.2.0/css/bootstrap-theme.min.css">
<script src="http://ajax.googleapis.com/ajax/libs/jquery/1.11.1/
jquery.min.js"></script>
<script src="http://maxcdn.bootstrapcdn.com/bootstrap/3.2.0/js/
bootstrap.min.js"></script>
<link rel="stylesheet" href="http://cdnjs.cloudflare.com/ajax/libs/
jasny-bootstrap/3.1.3/css/jasny-bootstrap.min.css">
```

```
<script src="http://cdnjs.cloudflare.com/ajax/libs/jasny-
bootstrap/3.1.3/js/jasny-bootstrap.min.js"></script>
</head>
<style> #packt { padding: 35px 35px 35px 35px;} </style>
<body id="packt"><br>
<!-- Standard button with label -->
<button type="button" class="btn btn-labeled btn-default"><span
class="btn-label"><i class="glyphicon glyphicon-arrow-left"></i></
span>Left</button>
<!-- Success button with label -->
<button type="button" class="btn btn-labeled btn-success"><span
class="btn-label"><i class="glyphicon glyphicon-ok"></i></
span>Success</button>
<!-- Danger button with label -->
<button type="button" class="btn btn-labeled btn-danger"><span
class="btn-label"><i class="glyphicon glyphicon-remove"></i></
span>Danger</button>
</body>
</html>
```

The output of this code upon execution will be as follows:

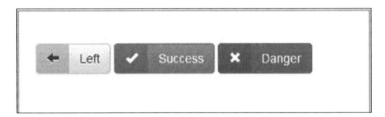

From the preceding code and the relevant output, it is quite obvious that the styling provided to the buttons results in the Glyphicons being used in conjunction with the buttons.

More information on Jasny Bootstrap can be found on its official website at http://jasny.github.io/bootstrap/.

Fuel UX

Fuel UX extends Bootstrap with JavaScript controls for your application without the bulk or noise. You can either download the files from the Git repository or use the CDN provided on the official website. Fuel UX has dependencies on jQuery and Bootstrap, therefore, you have to include these files before you include the link for the Fuel UX controls.

Take a look at the following code example to see how this works:

```
<!DOCTYPE html>
<html>
<head>
<title>Spinbox</title>
<meta name="viewport" content="width=device-width, initial-scale=1">
<link rel="stylesheet" href="http://maxcdn.bootstrapcdn.com/
bootstrap/3.2.0/css/bootstrap.min.css">
<link rel="stylesheet" href="http://maxcdn.bootstrapcdn.com/
bootstrap/3.2.0/css/bootstrap-theme.min.css">
<script src="http://ajax.googleapis.com/ajax/libs/jquery/1.11.1/
jquery.min.js"></script>
<script src="http://maxcdn.bootstrapcdn.com/bootstrap/3.2.0/js/
bootstrap.min.js"></script>
<link rel="stylesheet" href="http://www.fuelcdn.com/fuelux/3.0.2/css/
fuelux.min.css">
<script src="http://www.fuelcdn.com/fuelux/3.0.2/js/fuelux.min.js"></
script>
<style> .packt {padding: 50px 50px 50px 50px;} </style>
</head>
<body class="fuelux packt" >
<h1> Spinbox using Fuel UX </h1><br>
<div class="spinbox" data-initialize="spinbox" id="mySpinbox">
    <input type="text" class="form-control input-mini spinbox-input">
    <div class="spinbox-buttons btn-group btn-group-vertical">
      <button class="btn btn-primary spinbox-up btn-xs">
        <span class="glyphicon glyphicon-chevron-up"></span><span
class="sr-only">Increase</span>
      </button>
      <button class="btn btn-primary spinbox-down btn-xs">
```

```
        <span class="glyphicon glyphicon-chevron-down"></span><span
class="sr-only">Decrease</span>
        </button>
      </div>
    </div>
  </body>
</html>
```

The output of this code is as follows:

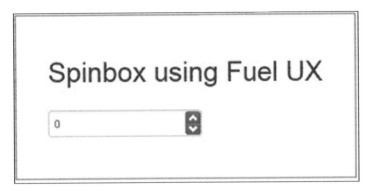

From the preceding output, you can see the spinbox, wherein you can increase and decrease the numeric count using the up and down arrow respectively.

More information about Fuel UX can be found on its official website at `http://exacttarget.github.io/fuelux/index.html`.

Bootsnipp

Bootsnipp (`http://bootsnipp.com/`) is an abundant library of free code snippets and design elements for the Bootstrap framework. It has snippets and samples related to various versions of Bootstrap. Once you click on the **Snippets** option in the menu bar, you will see a drop-down menu which has snippets according to the various versions of Bootstrap. Let's say we click on the **3.2.0** option. You will see all the ready-to-use examples.

Let's say we search for `Social Icon Strip Footer` by entering the same keywords in the search bar. Click on **View** and you will see the following screen and the corresponding URL would be `http://bootsnipp.com/snippets/featured/social-icon-strip-footer`:

In the screenshot, you can view the HTML and CSS files for **Social Icon Strip Footer**.

Apart from that, you can also select an alternative theme. One more thing to observe is that when you hover over any icon, it gets enlarged and the color changes as per the defined values in your code. Let's say we select the Cyborg theme and hover over the Google + icon. The theme gets applied and, on hovering over the Google+ icon, you will see the following screen:

More information and snippets can be found on the official website at
`http://bootsnipp.com/`.

Bootdey

Bootdey is a gallery of free snippets and utilities that you can use to streamline your web design with awesome accuracy. The utilities consist of plugins that you can incorporate in your projects and make your website more interactive and responsive, keeping in sync with the mobile-first approach.

Take a look at an example to understand it better. For the following example, we have chosen the **Social Post** snippet commonly used in blogs, the comments section, or on some Social Media platforms. You can either click on the **Social Post** link on the opening page or, alternatively, click on `http://www.bootdey.com/snippets/view/Social-post-222`:

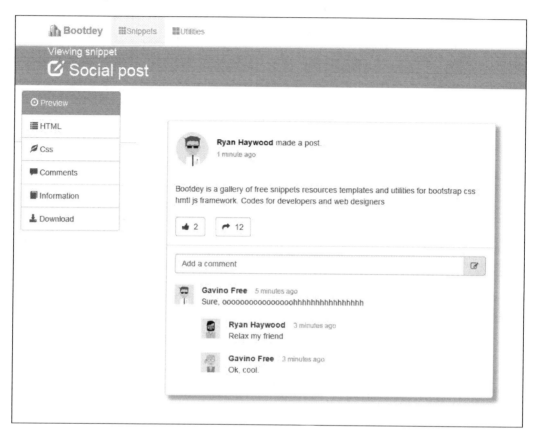

As you can see from the preceding screenshot, the left panel offers the **Preview**, **HTML**, **CSS**, **Comments**, **Information**, and **Download** options. If you click on the **HTML** option, you can view the entire HTML code for that example as depicted in the following screenshot:

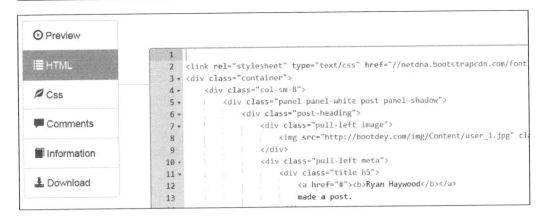

Thus, you can find a lot of tailor-made code for varied purposes ranging from a **Support Center** page to a gallery of plugins such as Easy Ticker, GMaps JQuery Map Plugin, and Freewall. These plugins will assist you in quick development of specific features, thereby allowing you to focus on the more imperative parts of your projects.

More information can be found on the official website: `http://bootdey.com/`.

BootBundle

BootBundle is a package of open source as well as commercial themes, templates, components, and other assets with attributes such as responsiveness and cross-browser compatibility. The BootBundle package can be downloaded from its official website (where you can see both free and open source packages) at `http://www.bootbundle.com/`.

Start Bootstrap

The Start Bootstrap website (`http://startbootstrap.com/bootstrap-resources/`) consists of all the plugins, resources, and development tools for Bootstrap. Ranging from common third-party Bootstrap jQuery plugins for Forms, Sliders, Tables, Menu, Navigation, Notifications, Modals, and other UI extensions, it is a one-stop hub for all Bootstrap resources.

Development tools and editors

In the previous sections, we took a look at the free and premium themes, templates, ready-made utilities, and plugins related to Bootstrap. We also saw the Start Bootstrap website that has the links to almost everything on Bootstrap. The Start Bootstrap website also has information about the development tools and editors used in web designing related to Bootstrap. In this section, we'll take a look at some of the popular development tools and editors which will significantly help you in your projects.

Bootply

Bootply is a Bootstrap code editor and builder that you can use to rapidly design and create interfaces with the drag-and-drop visual editor for Bootstrap. You can leverage the extensive code repository for snippets, examples, and templates. The following screenshot shows the interface for Bootply:

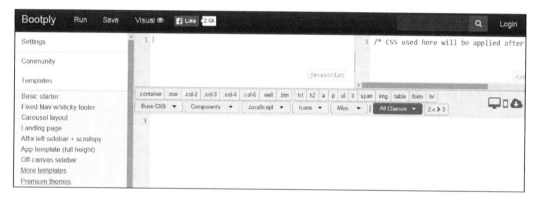

The preceding screenshot contains ready-made templates related to different versions of Bootstrap. Below the panel at the top of the screen, there is an on-the-fly preview screen that depicts the way your website will appear on updating as well as modification. You can save as well as fork the frontend you have built. The best part is that you can edit and customize the screen just the way you want it, thereby developing your frontend in no time. On the right side of the editor, there is a section that you can use to check how your web page will look on various devices such as tablet, desktop, or phone screens.

More information and attributes of Bootply can be found at:
`http://www.bootply.com/`.

LayoutIt

LayoutIt is a Bootstrap drag-and-drop editor that you can use to create frontend code. It easily integrates with any programming language, wherein you download the HTML code and start coding the design. You can customize it further by using your own LESS variables and loops, thereby helping you to build an accurate, impressive web page:

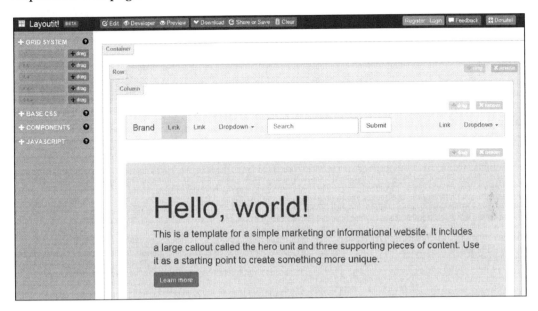

The preceding screenshot displays the builder and, as you can see on the left panel, there is **GRID SYSTEM** to choose the grid layout of your choice as well as use of several tailored CSS modules; components such as badges, jumbotron, and button groups; and JavaScript plugins such as modals and carousels in addition to customizing it with your own content. You have the developer tab and the preview tab for real-time display in addition to downloading the code in the .zip format with the choice of downloading the HTML only. This awesome utility helps you build your page in no time with precision and clarity.

More information can be found on its official website: http://www.layoutit.com/.

UI Bootstrap

UI Bootstrap incorporates Bootstrap components written in AngularJS by the AngularUI team. It aims to provide AngularJS directives with the markup and CSS of Bootstrap. It has dependencies on AngularJS and Bootstrap CSS.

More information can be found on its official website at `http://angular-ui.github.io/bootstrap/`.

Kickstrap

Kickstrap is a product where AngularJS is baked together with Bootstrap in conjunction with **JavaScript Package Manager (JSPM)**. You can leverage the advantage of running an authenticated database-driven web application without the native backend. Kickstrap uses Firebase adhering to a **Backend as a Service (BaaS)** model.

More information can be found on its official website at `http://getkickstrap.com/`.

ShoeStrap

ShoeStrap is an open source Wordpress theme based on Bootstrap and HTML5 Boilerplate. Its intuitive and powerful attributes make it one of the most widely-used and powerful Wordpress themes built on Bootstrap. You can also customize it using LESS snippets in addition to support from a vibrant community.

More information can be found on its official website at `http://shoestrap.org/`.

StrapPress

StrapPress is a toolkit that you can use to incorporate everything you get with Bootstrap, but with a focus on usability for Wordpress. It is a responsive Wordpress theme packed with a plethora of features that you can use to customize and create your own Wordpress site.

More information can be found on its official website at `http://strappress.com/`.

Summernote

Summernote is a lightweight yet effective WYSIWYG editor for Bootstrap. Its cross-platform nature, due to which you can integrate it with several backend technologies such as Ruby, PHP, and Python, makes it a handy tool for your projects.

More information can be found on its official website at
`http://hackerwins.github.io/summernote/`.

 As mentioned earlier, the entire suite of third-party resources, plugins, and toolkits can be found on the Start Bootstrap website at `http://startbootstrap.com/bootstrap-resources/`.

Official Bootstrap resources

There have been recent developments, due to which Bootstrap has evolved. All this can be found on the official Bootstrap blog at `http://blog.getbootstrap.com/`, helping you stay in sync with the latest updates.

Let's take a look at some of the resources and relevant information on the official web page.

Bootlint

The Bootlint utility is an HTML linting tool for projects using Vanilla Bootstrap and can be implemented at the browser level or from the terminal using Node.js. Thus you can automatically check for common Bootstrap usage errors. You can also use Bootlint with Grunt, which is a JavaScript task runner. You can check the entire project at `https://github.com/twbs/bootlint`, which leads to the GitHub page, wherein you avail the latest updates and the usage instructions.

Bootstrap with SaaS

Bootstrap with SaaS is a handy resource, which is just the correct implementation for SaaS-powered applications. Compass, an open source CSS preprocessor, uses SaaS, and its combination with Bootstrap helps you build a completely responsive website in no time, in addition to helping you write lightweight, programmable, and maintainable CSS. A major development was the inclusion of Bootstrap-powered SaaS in the Rails project as well as other SaaS-powered projects.

The recent updates, as well as the official SaaS port of Bootstrap, can be found on the official GitHub platform at `https://github.com/twbs/bootstrap-sass`.

Bootstrap Expo

The Bootstrap Expo (`http://expo.getbootstrap.com/`) is the official directory for websites and web applications being developed by the framework. You can also showcase your website (*terms and conditions apply*) on the Expo.

Summary

In this chapter, we had an overview of all the additional toolkits and commodities that streamline web designing with Bootstrap. The latest exciting development, according to the Bootstrap Blog, is the launch of Ratchet 2.0.2 (`http://goratchet.com/`), a mobile-only framework developed by the team at Bootstrap that helps you build mobile apps with a native feel. Bootstrap is an innovation with reusable modules combined with great extensibility and sensible defaults. Bootstrap's platform-agnostic nature and flexibility, in addition to a vibrant community, makes it one of the most prevalent frameworks in 2014. As Bootstrap grows, so does its scope and myriad combinations. The latest version of Joomla comes with Bootstrap support. Wordpress is compatible with Bootstrap and supports it completely. Python has integrated Bootstrap in its library package. With the advent of mobile devices and smart telephony, Bootstrap seems set to become a vital cog in the wheel for accurate and rapid futuristic web design.

Index

Thank you for buying
Learning Bootstrap

About Packt Publishing

Packt, pronounced 'packed', published its first book, *Mastering phpMyAdmin for Effective MySQL Management*, in April 2004, and subsequently continued to specialize in publishing highly focused books on specific technologies and solutions.

Our books and publications share the experiences of your fellow IT professionals in adapting and customizing today's systems, applications, and frameworks. Our solution-based books give you the knowledge and power to customize the software and technologies you're using to get the job done. Packt books are more specific and less general than the IT books you have seen in the past. Our unique business model allows us to bring you more focused information, giving you more of what you need to know, and less of what you don't.

Packt is a modern yet unique publishing company that focuses on producing quality, cutting-edge books for communities of developers, administrators, and newbies alike. For more information, please visit our website at www.packtpub.com.

About Packt Open Source

In 2010, Packt launched two new brands, Packt Open Source and Packt Enterprise, in order to continue its focus on specialization. This book is part of the Packt Open Source brand, home to books published on software built around open source licenses, and offering information to anybody from advanced developers to budding web designers. The Open Source brand also runs Packt's Open Source Royalty Scheme, by which Packt gives a royalty to each open source project about whose software a book is sold.

Writing for Packt

We welcome all inquiries from people who are interested in authoring. Book proposals should be sent to author@packtpub.com. If your book idea is still at an early stage and you would like to discuss it first before writing a formal book proposal, then please contact us; one of our commissioning editors will get in touch with you.

We're not just looking for published authors; if you have strong technical skills but no writing experience, our experienced editors can help you develop a writing career, or simply get some additional reward for your expertise.

Mobile First Bootstrap

ISBN: 978-1-78328-579-2   Paperback: 92 pages

Develop advanced websites optimized for mobile devices using the Mobile First feature of Bootstrap

1. Get to grips with the essentials of mobile-first development with Bootstrap.

2. Understand the entire process of building a mobile-first website with Bootstrap from scratch.

3. Packed with screenshots that help guide you through how to build an appealing website from a mobile-first perspective with the help of a real-world example.

Bootstrap Site Blueprints

ISBN: 978-1-78216-452-4   Paperback: 304 pages

Design mobile-first responsive websites with Bootstrap 3

1. Learn the inner workings of Bootstrap 3 and create web applications with ease.

2. Quickly customize your designs working directly with Bootstrap's LESS files.

3. Leverage Bootstrap's excellent JavaScript plugins.

Please check **www.PacktPub.com** for information on our titles

Extending Bootstrap

ISBN: 978-1-78216-841-6   Paperback: 88 pages

Understand Bootstrap and unlock its secrets to build a truly customized project!

1. Learn to use themes to improve your user experience.

2. Improve your workflow with LESS and Grunt.js.

3. Get to know the most useful third-party Bootstrap plugins.

Building a Responsive Website with Bootstrap [Video]

ISBN: 978-1-78216-498-2   Duration: 1:56 hours

Build unique and responsive business layouts using modern techniques with Twitter Bootstrap

1. Implement incredible Bootstrap-only features such as the grid, image carousel, and more.

2. Use Retina-ready icon fonts to make your site look awesome.

3. Learn time-saving tips and tricks to optimize your site's performance.

Please check **www.PacktPub.com** for information on our titles

Made in the USA
San Bernardino, CA
25 July 2015